*Un-*SPECIAL NEEDS

BEV LINDER

Un-SPECIAL NEEDS

There's More To Your Child
Than "Special Needs"!

Published by Special Heart

© 2014 by Bev Linder

Cover Design by Arvid Wallen
RAWcreativity
Woodland Park, Colorado

ISBN: 978-0-692-26829-2

Note to Reader: The ideas and suggestions contained in this book are not intended as a substitute for appropriate care of a licensed health care practitioner

This book is dedicated to my husband Michael, who has always encouraged me to spread my wings in pursuing new challenges, and who has been a most remarkable dad to our three precious children.

Contents

Acknowledgments

We didn't really try to form a "team" of people who were wholly committed to the endeavor of this book, of touching the lives of families with kids who have special needs. But to our astonishment, as Mike and I worked on gathering gifted individuals who could make the various parts of this book happen, we realized that we had found more than competent contributors, but God seemed to be working in the hearts of each one of these men and women so that this project was something meaningful from their hearts.

Karen Leonard who contributed to chapter 5 and who along with her husband Jim, wrote the Workbook/Leader's Guide—prayed endlessly that God would use our efforts to touch the lives of special families. When she took the manuscript of the book along to work on during her family vacation for a trip up the coast, I knew for certain that Karen's heart was bound to this endeavor! Thank you, Karen, for always signing your notes with "Onward!"

Arvid Wallen, a gifted designer, amazed Mike and me when he offered to create the book cover for *Un-Special Needs*, but amazed us even more when we met him for lunch to discuss the final decisions, and he informed us that he had just returned from the cemetery where Brad is laid to rest. He lives in the same town as this little mountain cemetery. He found a bench and sat there and prayed "for Brad's legacy" in this book. We knew then that this was more than an art project for him; it was something that God had laid on his heart to be part of. Mike and I are thankful for you, Arvid.

Karen Cooper, not only scanned some of the chapters with a mom's eye and an editor's discernment, but asked her kids, one of whom is a teen who has autism, to evaluate the different sections of the book, particularly the KIDZ section. This was above and beyond her call of duty, demonstrating that her heart was deeply into this project. And how helpful to have the actual kids to whom this section is addressed give their input and evaluation. Thank you to Ian, Julia, and Kyle for helping so much, even in pointing out the different pros and cons for the cover choices!

Darla Hightower proofread the book. I saw that same team spirit in her when she said that she wanted to be part of what the book might accomplish in helping both kids and parents. I'm grateful for your tender heart, Darla.

*Ange Smith...*how can I thank you for the faith you and your entire family have inspired in my own heart and in the hearts of many others! Ange and Gorden live in Zimbabwe and have fought the good fight in helping their daughter Amy get treatment and help for her life-threatening condition. Amy herself is an inspiration to my own faith. She seems to often dwell with her heart above her circumstances, singing when we expect her to be mourning her situation, thinking about others when we would expect her to be thinking of herself. I'm grateful that Ange allowed us to get a peek of her struggles and victories of faith in chapter 3.

Anne Marie Ezzo has been an encourager always. She is a model of a godly woman with a gentle and quiet spirit, and has been a source of many years of wisdom to me personally in all areas of life. I am grateful for your friendship, Anne Marie, and for your caring heart.

Tia Smith went way beyond "the call of duty" in making sure every jot and tittle of the book made sense. She mentioned several times how glad she was to be part of this project—and how glad we are that she has been part of it!

My son Ricky has encouraged and cheered on, writing me emails like the following on days when I wondered if I could keep going writing this book: "Mom, you are offering something unique, and if anybody has the credibility to see good in hard times, it's you." Thank you, Ricky. You'll never know how much I have been strengthened by your words of support!

Foreword

Once I finally overcame the shock of my child's "special" diagnosis and began the process of coping, understanding, and embracing, I searched everywhere for help. As I sifted through the resources on the Internet, I remember my frustration with all of the "empathy" sites. Not that there's anything wrong with empathy. I appreciate those who are bold enough to share the highs and lows of their journey, and I can totally identify with the need to know "you're not alone." But I was looking for something more.

Then one morning I came across a resource that was different. It looked the same—a website authored by a special mom offering stories and counsel. But within her words I found a rare commodity—hope! This was the beginning of my journey following the encouraging words of Beverly Linder. Over the next few years I would delight when the Special Heart email hit my inbox. It brought a ray of sunshine to my day, not because her writing was only about happy times, but because it was never helpless or hopeless. It often challenged me to another level of responsibility and a few of them even made me a little uncomfortable.

Being made to feel just slightly uncomfortable is actually what I love about this book you hold in your hands! If you have no desire to break out of the status quo, then this may not be the right reading material for you. The following chapters are brimming with concepts that had never occurred to me, and that no one else brought to my attention. Through the years of being a special mom, I found that I sort of settled into a niche. I don't think I'm the only one. I see a lot of special parents whose identity is wrapped up in their child's disability. We who truly embrace the role often wear it as a badge of honor. It's a wonderful acceptance, but also a dangerous pitfall. We very rarely are corrected or challenged in our parenting (who would dare?), and although we are always advocating for our child's growth and progress, we would have to admit we neglect our own growth and progress—at least as far as being a special parent is concerned.

Bev Linder is probably one of the few people in the world who has the credibility (as a parent of two special children and one typical child) combined with the courage to challenge us parents of special kids. Please don't misunderstand—this book is going to encourage you about the great job you're doing. But it is also going to challenge you to see every area of your special parenting duties in a new light, in an un-special light, perhaps for the first time.

The uniqueness of this book is that it shows us that we are also called to be "typical" parents, because each of our special kids longs to be a typical child. This simple revelation alone within the first few pages of the book brought me to tears— sweet tears of acknowledgment. I see this desire to simply be a kid each day in my fourteen-year-old son, but never gave it enough weight. Our busy schedule of therapies, behavior modification routines, homeschool, and (heaven forbid) a little "mommy time" leaves very little room for un-special kid stuff.

Although my child and Bev's (and probably yours) couldn't be more different in their challenges, the same universal truth of un-special needs resonates in every chapter. I will admit that on every page lies a fairly obvious need that I had somehow missed or disregarded for my son. Bev goes beyond theory by also providing strategies to intentionally address many of these issues in a practical way. Even with the most profoundly challenged child, an impact can be made.

This book isn't all about un-special needs; it also addresses the reality of special needs. The wrap-up of the book is my favorite, where Bev points out so beautifully something I had never considered: "The moment a child is diagnosed with a special condition, at that moment his parents also come to have special needs that other parents don't have." Bev lays out our very special needs, and shows us how our loving Heavenly Father is waiting to meet those needs very uniquely for us.

I finished *Un-Special Needs* feeling encouraged and empowered. I am excited to shift my parenting focus to the most un-special of my son's needs, areas where I now place much greater intentionality and emphasis. I pray that you too will be encouraged and that through these chapters of wisdom, you will hear your Heavenly Father speaking directly to your heart and into your one-of-a-kind parenting adventure.

Melanie Gomez
Christian counselor, MS
Special mom

www.RedefineSpecial.com

Kids Were Made to Fly!

"OH, oh, oh! Let's go fly a kite, up to the highest height!" I can still see and hear my daughter Kristie singing that song at the top of her little lungs as she sat watching a music video in her specially made chair so that she could be upright.

She was two years old at the time, and my mind reflected in wonder, remembering the day she was born, when my husband and I were told that she would never talk and that her mental faculties would be quite limited. Boy, they got that wrong! Not only did Kristie sing, but she chattered incessantly.

But the doctors were right about her physical condition. Kristie was as "floppy" as a rag doll, her muscles being profoundly low in tone. She couldn't walk, and it was difficult for her to even lift her head.

My "mom's heart" knew why she wanted to watch that Disney music video over and over. When she sang about flying a kite, her spirit would soar above the clouds, her limitations would be for that moment nonexistent, and the person who lived inside that weak and disabled body, would fly!

Kristie would sometimes say, "Mama, someday I will walk; someday I will dance; someday I will fly like Peter Pan!"

When she left us for heaven at age three due to a serious respiratory illness, I remembered her words, and my heart rejoiced that her "someday" had come, though the hole in our lives was beyond description.

Kristie left behind her one-year-old brother, Ricky, who did not have any limitations or special needs. When he was four or five, he loved to go to a field of tall grass with his butterfly net and run his little legs off, capturing butterflies to put in a jar to take home for observation. As I watched him nearly fly through that field with such gleeful squeals of joy, I was reminded that *all* children love for their spirit to soar. Kristie and Ricky had different abilities, but they had the same needs and desires in their spirit, ones that God Himself put there.

Then when Ricky was four years old, his brother Bradley was born. We were crushed to find that Brad had the same basic muscle disorder that Kristie had, only it manifested itself in a more severe way. Brad's fingers and feet were noticeably twisted, and during the first few months, he didn't seem to have the ability to show forth his personality. Unlike Kristie, he didn't utter a word until he was four years old! To top it off, he was a grouchy baby, and we had never had a grouchy baby before. But who wouldn't be grouchy? From the time he was born, Brad had broken bones, he needed surgery, he was poked by needles. Yes, Brad had plenty of reasons to be out of sorts.

Still, as the months went by, we began to detect that same spirit that was present in our other two children, even though it almost had to show itself through the cracks, so to speak, of Brad's broken body. He began to smile. He began to relate. He began to show determination and a desire to reach beyond his limitations. His body couldn't restrain the spirit that was inside, that spirit of a kid made in the image of God and made, like all kids, to take to the air in their spirit.

I remember thinking about this when Brad was a young teen. He had become a good drummer, and that night his parents, his brother, and his grandparents had come to watch him be part of a band concert. The band did well, and at the end of the performance, the audience began to applaud. All the band members stood to their feet in response to the roaring appreciation, and as his family members watched in horror of what might happen, Brad planted his feet on the ground and decided that he must stand with the others! He fell backward to the chair, and fortunately not forward to the ground, and our hearts broke that he could not take his well-deserved bow.

But at that moment, I knew that Brad was more aware of his soaring spirit than he was of his limited body; he wanted to fly. And fly he did, but in a different way. He flew way higher than the kids who were able to stand up, for as he was thrust back into that chair, he chose to have joy that evening in spite of his limitations.

Bradley left us for the same Home his sister Kristie had when he was eighteen years old.

Is this book, *Un-Special Needs*, about flying? In a way. It is a book of tools for parents of kids who have special needs to help them meet their children's needs, the needs they have that are common to all young people, and in so doing, to release their spirit to be all that they were created to be.

I recently went to a memorial service of a young woman of thirty-five years who passed away after a four-year battle with cancer. She lived much longer than expected, according to her initial diagnosis. After two years, Heather said, "There's more to me than cancer," and, "God has given me life, I'm going to live it." Although some had begun to define Heather by her cancer, she knew that her cancer was not basic to who she was.

Heather did not have special needs, but her words reflect the spirit of this book, for there is more to your special-needs child than special needs! This book is an encouragement to not give in to the pull to define your child by his or her disability or any form of what we call "special needs."

The cry of your child's heart, whether or not he or she is able to express it, is "Please see the person I am! There is so much more to me than my disability!"

And in essence, these young people know deep in their soul that although they have special needs, they have more un-special needs, because they are so much more than what others might see on the outside—for people tend to get distracted and focus on the problem rather than the person!

This book is not about flying in the sense that it is pie-in-the-sky. No, each chapter is very rubber-meets-the-road practical. But it is about flying in the sense of releasing this child, whom others may be tempted to define as a problem, to spread his wings, so to speak, and to have the attitude of "God has given me life, and I am going to live it!"

Structure of the Book

I have a confession to make: I am sometimes an introduction skipper! That is, I will dive right into a book without reading the introduction. I hope that you, having read this far, will continue reading because understanding some of the elements that make up each chapter of the book will be immensely helpful to you to get the most out of it.

There are three parts to each chapter, two of which are focused on application. There is the main body of the chapter; then there is the "Time to Soar"; and finally there is the "KIDZ" section.

Feel free to use or not use the Time to Soar and the KIDZ sections according to your needs. Time to Soar offers a number of practical suggestions for application related to the content of the chapter. You may look it over and pick and choose whatever suggestions might be helpful to you. It is for the purpose of putting some "shoe leather" on the chapter content that might otherwise be left un-applied. And we all know that application is what makes a book worth reading!

The KIDZ section was a little iffy to write. There are so very many variations of special needs and degrees of abilities and disabilities that it is impossible to address every young person exactly where they are. Some kids can pick it up and read the material themselves. Some can listen while their parents read. Some may need for their parents to translate the material in a way that only parents who understand the unique learning style of their children can do. Some may seem not to be able to understand the content at all. But I'm hoping that you as a parent will be able to read the KIDZ section and take the parts that your child will benefit from, as well as communicate the material in a way that he or she will be able to assimilate and apply. Some young people may be physically or cognitively unable to try many of the suggestions. Please seek to modify the suggestions in a way that can apply to your child. I believe that the applications for the kids are worth some effort in communicating them, even if it takes creativity on your part to do so!

Even though writing this section was iffy in the sense of how could I ever relate to such a wide variety of kids, I took the challenge *because I found that I had a desire in my heart to not just talk about the kids, but to talk to them.*

Although we had three children and enjoyed each one uniquely and completely, it is Bradley that you will see mentioned most often as an illustration. The reason for that is Kristie was only with us three years and therefore didn't leave as many memories and experiences for us to relate. Ricky, not having special needs, will be mentioned, but because his life was more typical, most of his experiences don't lend themselves to a discussion in the topic of this book. So it is Brad whom you will become most acquainted with. Nevertheless, we are equally grateful for all three of our children who so enriched our lives!

My prayer for you and your family is that God will touch your lives, even if in just a small way, through the pages of this book, and that the soul of your child will be a little freer to fly!

One can never consent to creep,
when one feels an impulse to soar.
HELEN KELLER

I Need a Sense of Purpose

*The mystery of human existence
lies not in just staying alive
but in finding something to live for.*

FYODOR DOSTOEVSKY, The Brothers Karamazov

*I came that they may have life,
and have it abundantly.*

JESUS, John 10:10

We all need to know that there is a reason, a purpose for taking up space in this world.

It isn't surprising that we feel this compelling need to know that we matter. God has put this drive in our hearts to make a difference, to touch lives, to use our snowflake-like, one-of-a-kind gifts to make an impression on this world in a way that no one else is able, because no one else was created with exactly the same style of expressing the image of God.

It is an un-special need to know that my life is not an accident, but rather that there is a purpose devised in the heart and mind of God, for my being alive.

But something tragic can happen when a person has a significant disability of any kind. There is a tendency for that person to feel, many times because of the way others treat him, that he is in survival mode—that is, that his only purpose is to deal with his limitations and to try to survive the daily struggles of having needs that are harder-than-average.

Believe me, I know from raising my kids that indeed huge amounts of time and energy do go into meeting special needs. But as parents of special kids, we need to always keep in the forefront of our minds that God desires for this child to leave a fingerprint on our world, a fingerprint that demonstrates something of His character, and in some way reveals what He is like.

In John chapter 9, the disciples asked Jesus, "Who sinned, this man or his parents, that he would be born blind?" They were looking for a human cause. But Jesus passed over any human cause and went right into the purpose of God in allowing the man's blindness saying, "It was neither that this man sinned, nor his parents; but it was so that the works of God might be displayed in him" (verses 1-3). In this case, "the works of God" was the healing of the man. But healing is not always how God displays His works in individuals with disabilities. He does so in a variety of ways. Haven't you noticed how a child with special needs can capture the attention and the heart of those who are exposed to his life?

I'll tell you an amazing conclusion that I have come to after being immersed in the world of disability for so long: *Individuals who have difficult challenges of any sort are more, not less, equipped to make a dramatic and lasting impression on people and are therefore more, not less, qualified to impact this world in a positive way.*

No One Left Out

I think I can "hear" what might be your objections. What about the autistic child who has such a difficult time relating at all to others? What about the child who has a cognitive and/or physical disability that causes him so often to be left out and left behind? And what about the child who may have such all-encompassing limitations that she needs total care and it is nearly impossible to even leave the house most of the time?

Good questions. It can be confusing when we see an individual with special needs struggling with accomplishing the basics of life each day. But we have to look deeper than what we see on the surface. In Jeremiah chapter 1 God says to the prophet, "Before I formed you in the womb I knew you, and before you were born I consecrated you; I have appointed you a prophet to the nations" (verse 5). Similarly, the apostle Paul said in Galatians 1:15 that God had set him apart before he was born and called him to the purpose for which He created him.

Now the question is, are only prophets and apostles set apart by God for His purposes? The answer is found in Ephesians 2:10 where in speaking about all God's children it says, "We are God's handiwork, created in Christ Jesus to do good works, which God prepared in advance for us to do" (NIV).

Clearly the Creator has a purpose for each individual before he is born and which God desires that he discover and live out. Now here's another question: If God has a purpose for each of His children to touch the world and to reveal His own character in a unique way, is that only for completely healthy people? Does it exclude the person who has limitations and what we call "special needs"?

The answer has to be, of course not! In fact, those who appear to be "weak" are described by God as specially chosen for His good purposes. First Corinthians 1:27 says that God chose what is weak in the world to shame the strong. And likewise in 2 Corinthians 12:9 when Paul asks God to remove a "thorn in the flesh," which appears to be a limitation or disability of some kind, God answers, "power is perfected in weakness."

So what does that all look like in real life? It looks like real individuals touching their world in a real way, not *in spite of* their limitations, but amazingly, often *because of* them! The purpose does not always need to be "spiritual." As your child grows in a relationship with his Creator, in time, the purposes that he attaches himself to will become God-directed and eternally valuable.

Balancing Special Needs and Un-Special Needs

Imagine going to a doctor for help with your child who is not developing in a typical way and having that doctor tell you that your child is autistic, that it is your fault for some flaw in your parenting, and that you need to institutionalize her because she can never improve...all in one appointment! Such was the experience of Temple Grandin's mom in the early 1950s.

Temple's mom had a dose of God-given "mom common sense" and left the office determined to bring out the person who she knew was "in there," in the soul of her daughter. She set her face like flint to help her daughter participate in a positive way in her world.

In an interview with the Autism Research Institute, Temple said, "You have got to keep autistic children engaged in the world. You cannot let them tune out."[1] And that was her mom's foundation for her decisions with Temple—she would not let her tune out from the world that she knew held promise for Temple finding purpose in life.

It was a slow-go during those years when so many would gladly write off the little girl with autism as someone who had nothing to offer.

Temple describes her experience of being nonverbal: "I can remember the frustration of not being able to talk. I knew what I wanted to say, but I could not get the words out, so I would scream." Temple was nonverbal until around age four.

To make a very long and fascinating story short, Temple's disability not only became her greatest strength, but her autism and her unique way of focusing intensely, in her case, on animal behavior, benefited the world of animal husbandry beyond what anyone who knew her as a child could have ever imagined.

According to her website: "Dr. Temple Grandin is a designer of livestock handling facilities and an Associate Professor of Animal Science at Colorado State University. In North America, almost half the cattle are handled in a center track restrainer system that she designed for meat plants."[2]

I've been fascinated by Temple's story. Sure, not every young person who has autism or some other special issue is going to become a college professor nor become world renowned for his or her achievements. But Temple discovered a meaningful purpose for her life even within her very real limitations, and I believe her mom had a huge part in nurturing the right kind of environment for her daughter to grow. As I read what Temple says about her childhood, I see a mom who skillfully balanced her daughter's special needs with her un-special needs.

In a recent interview with Family Action Network, Temple summarized the tenets that both she and her now eighty-seven-year-old mom share with thousands of people (yes, her mom is apparently a quite eloquent speaker still!). Following are just a few of the principles that she shared in the interview:

"We need to teach social skills like parents taught me and

others in the '50s: how to shop, shake hands, order food, look at someone when you talk to them.

"Sensory issues—like hypersensitivity to sound, smells or touch are a very real problem. Teach kids to control what bothers them and they will improve.

"Parents need to let their children struggle more. Let them tackle problems that interest them and fail. The worst moments of our lives can define the best that will come.

"When kids do work that others will want, their social skills improve too. Don't let them become recluses in their rooms playing video games."[3]

I see a balance in Temple's words, a recognition that there are difficult issues to tackle. For Temple, one of those was her hypersensitivity due to her autism. Yet, there is a constant nudging forward into the typical world. This is hard for parents, especially moms. I speak from experience. It is heartrending to watch your child have to struggle so greatly in life with activities and interactions that seem to come so easily for others. But purpose can be found for kids in getting "out there," with much support from parents, and tackling the typical life skills, such as the ones mentioned above by Temple that will help them find their niche in the world. The ability to do that will vary greatly from one type of special need to another, but the principle is the same—to keep nudging forward according to the abilities and potential abilities of the child.

Daily Purpose

"What are you up to Mom?" That is often my greeting when I call my eighty-nine-year-old mother to see how she is doing. I'm always afraid of hearing some bad news, since she is getting up there in age. But that day, she answered the phone more cheerfully than usual. "I'm making pizzelles (Italian waffle cookies) for my eye doctor since I have an appointment with him this week and he loves those cookies!"

When we talk about having a sense of purpose, there is the kind of purpose that leaves a mark on the world, and then there is the kind of daily purpose that individuals need in order to stay motivated and engaged in life. That day my mom had a project, a goal, something she was doing to make someone else happy, something she was good at, and that brought her fulfillment. She had a purpose for that day.

So it is with special kids. I think of my friend Vicki who homeschools her two children, one of whom has Down syndrome. Steven's case of Down's leaves him nonverbal. His cognitive scores are low.

But anyone who walks into Steven's presence is greeted with sparkling eyes and a big hug, along with an attempt at a cheerful and heartfelt verbal greeting. I believe that Vicki and her husband Tom's perseverance in keeping Steven occupied with daily, interesting projects greatly contributes to his spunky spirit. In fact, although Steven is nonverbal, Vicki taught him to read three-letter words with sign language and puzzles. I personally could not hold back my tears when Steven demonstrated his abilities to me with glowing face and ear-to-ear grin, looking up often to make sure that I was as impressed as I should be. And impressed I was!

It's the kind of thing where you walk away saying to yourself, "If Steven can persevere in that way, surely I can persevere in my challenges!" And that, in fact, is a common way that God uses individuals with disabilities. They have a way of acting as a silent rebuke and at the same time an inspiration to those of us who complain about how difficult our lives are.

Granted, it is often puzzling, even befuddling, to discover how to stimulate and engage a child who has cognitive and other issues. Yet, I encourage you to adopt the old adage, "where there's a will, there's a way," knowing that there is a person in there with a need to be guided into ways of expressing his un-special need of having a purpose each day.

It is often a matter of taking God at His word, in spite of the seeming contradiction of what our eyes tell us as we watch these precious ones struggle each day. But turn your eyes of faith to what God says, that He uniquely created this child for a good purpose, and that realizing this truth and helping your child realize it will bring a new perspective, a fresh kind of energy to you, to your child, and to the rest of your family.

Yes, it takes time; yes, it takes energy (two resources that "special parents" are already low on!), but you are helping the soul of your child to thrive when you provide activities other than constant electronics—such as crafts, helping in the kitchen, and problem-solving games on their level.

There have been many times in my own life when I felt like Eeyore—like I was way down in the dumps; and at those times, finding something to engage my mind, body, and soul has almost magically lifted me out of the slump. That's the way we are all wired, special kids included.

It is an un-special need to have daily, interesting activities that keep me active and engaged in expressing my gifts and in being involved with making a contribution to my family and others beyond my family.

What About the Cognitively Challenged?

"Don't think that Katie can't take in just because it is difficult for her to give out." I'll never forget those words to me from my friend Sharon whom I lived with some years ago for six weeks. Theirs was a happy, lively family, and Katie, who had, as her mom described it at the time, "profound CP," would join all family meals and activities. Her parents would put food in her mouth and then cover it so that the food would go down. Katie would not, in fact, could not, focus on a person's face. Yet, when her mom sang to her and told her about hope in Jesus, she would break out in a grin with sparkling eyes.

There's no denying that such individuals pose a mystery to us, as we wonder how much they are actually taking in. But why miss the opportunity to communicate with them when there is a good chance that indeed they may be taking in more than we think?

Many individuals who appear to be unable to understand have proven otherwise over time. One such person is Carly Fleischmann. An interesting report came out with ABC news a few years back about Carly, a teenager who has a degree of Autism that has made her nonverbal and prone to unsettling expressions of frustration, such as banging her head on the floor. She was a complete mystery to her parents until one amazing day when she was eleven years old, she walked over to the typewriter in a therapy session and typed out a message, having never done anything like that before! From that point on, her parents encouraged her to type her thoughts. What is and has been in Carly's head is astounding! She types messages like, "It is hard to be autistic because no one understands me. People look at me and assume I am dumb because I can't speak."

Her parents have been on an emotional roller coaster! In response to a question to her dad about how he felt when he discovered Carly's comprehension ability, he said, "We were horrified because for years we had spoken in front of her as if she wasn't there."[3]

Admittedly, there are all sorts and levels of cognitive disability in a variety of conditions. Still, to tell a young person of her purpose in life, no matter what form of intellectual challenge she may have, may well be received and processed by her. Give her a chance, and speak the truth to her about God's intentional design for her life. Perhaps begin by reading or paraphrasing Psalm 139 to her.

"Neither Useless nor Unfruitful..."

There are kids who have limitations that are so pronounced that life seems to be on the level of survival for them. How do these young people find purpose in their lives?

There's a fascinating promise written by Peter in his second letter. In this passage, Peter lists character qualities such as diligence, perseverance, brotherly kindness, and self-control. Then he makes this profound observation: "If these qualities are yours and are increasing, they render you *neither useless nor unfruitful*" (1:5-8, italics mine).

Joni Eareckson Tada has commented that this passage has given her strength when she felt like her paralyzed body was a hindrance to her fruitfulness.

I have a friend who refers to her daughter as "total care." Although she is a teenager, she must be fed, bathed, her bathroom needs met—she constantly needs someone to meet her basic needs and much of my friend's life is spent in the meeting of those needs.

How does the idea of finding purpose in life relate to young people in this position?

My son Brad was not total care; although his disability was great, he was able to be out and about. Yet, because of his many illnesses, hospital stays, and surgeries, he was in a position of total care a good deal of the time, being often too weak to even feed himself. So we have had a chance, my husband and I being his caregivers, to observe close-up and personal how God can make such a life full of purpose.

I woke up this morning with a memory that made me smile. We were in San Diego for one of Brad's more grueling surgeries. He was probably around twelve years old at the time and had just that day gotten to the point where he could very weakly sit in a wheelchair. We had recently watched a silly movie called *Galaxy Quest*, which is a spoof on *Star Trek*. In it, one of the characters would clench his fist and draw it to his breast and say, "Never give up; never surrender."

When Brad finally got into his wheelchair at the hospital, I left for a moment down a long hallway to use the restroom. When I came out, I could see Brad, way down there, and he had brought his fist to his breast in a motion to me, which said, "Never give up; never surrender." I did the motion back, and we stood there for a moment with our fists on our hearts, pausing to give each other the message that we would indeed never give up.

That memory of Brad sending that hopeful message down the hallway of Children's Hospital was a reminder to me that a child can have a sense of purpose, even while in a position of complete vulnerability and weakness that keeps him from performing the simplest tasks in life without assistance. Why? Because it is during life's most difficult times that a person can inspire others by demonstrating that the human spirit can be resilient and full of courage. The qualities mentioned by Peter in the verse above can be more, not less, on display in a person who is so limited on the outside, yet unhindered to display fortitude and perseverance on the inside...and can you think of a more meaningful life purpose than that?

Time to Soar

Verbalize life-giving messages.

Pleasant words are a honeycomb, sweet to the soul and healing to the bones.
Proverbs 16:24

Would you like to bring a kind of healing to the soul of your child? This proverb promises that words bring healing, and sometimes can even touch the "bones," that is, the body, in a healthful way!

I have seen this kind of healing happen before my eyes when I have verbalized affirming words to my children such as:

"I'm so glad that God made you, and I like you just the way you are."

"I'm looking forward to seeing how God uses your life now, and as you grow up."

"I know that God is going to bless other people through the gifts and talents He has given you."

"There is no one else in this world like you, and I'm so glad you are part of our family!"

"I wouldn't trade you for any kid in the world!"

You may be thinking that all children need to hear comments

like these from their parents. Indeed they do! But it is especially rare for parents to say these kinds of words of purpose to the child who has special needs.

Or maybe you're thinking that you can't say these things because you don't feel that way and it would be dishonest. But look at it another way: Sometimes we say and do things "by faith," even if our feelings aren't there at first. If you look your kids in the eye and say these kinds of affirming words to them based on your faith in God's Word, your feelings will likely follow, and you just might be amazed at the changes you see in your kids, and in yourself! Yours will be pleasant, healing words to your children.

*Let God do the talking!

Maybe you don't know quite what to say to impress on your child that his life is full of purpose. Let God do the talking through His Word!

God has written us a love letter, a guide, and an encouragement to find the daily purpose He has for us. It's no different for the special child. He needs that Word which claims to be "a lamp to my feet and a light to my path" (Psalm 119:105).

Following are some verses that address the issue of *purpose*. Why not have a time each day, say at breakfast, when a few of these are read out loud? As mentioned before, if you think your special child can't understand, read to them anyway. Go on the assumption that there may be more understanding than you realize.

> The LORD will fulfill his purpose for me; your steadfast love, O LORD, endures forever.
> Psalm 138:8 (ESV)

I can do all things through Him who strengthens me.
Philippians 4:13

The conclusion, when all has been heard, is: fear God and keep His commandments, because this applies to every person.
Ecclesiastes 12:13

Whatever you do in word or deed, do all in the name of the Lord Jesus, giving thanks through Him to God the Father.
Colossians 3:17

So teach us to number our days, that we may present to You a heart of wisdom.
Psalm 90:12

Whether, then, you eat or drink or whatever you do, do all to the glory of God.
1 Corinthians 10:31

He has told you, O man, what is good; and what does the LORD require of you but to do justice, to love kindness, and to walk humbly with your God?
Micah 6:8

But as many as received Him, to them He gave the right to become children of God, even to those who believe in His name.
John 1:12

*Check out resources.

Do2Learn (www.do2learn.com) is a resource for kids with special needs that has tons of materials, some of it free! This kind of thing is ideal for the homeschooling parent, but even if your child goes to school during the day, don't leave his development entirely to the professionals! Keep his mind and his hands active with constructive activities at home as well.

*Pray.

Suggested prayer for your child: (For the sake of simplicity, after the first sentence in the prayer, the pronoun used will be masculine.)

> Dear Lord,
> My child does so need to know that You have created him/her for a wonderful purpose. Help him see beyond the problems and past the limitations to the true person who lives inside. I know that it will be easier for him to do that if his parents see that person within him that You have made and that You have created for Your good purposes. Help me as a parent to see and affirm the value in my child each day. And help him to see that value in himself so that he may know that life is more than survival; rather it is an adventure of living out Your will for his life. I pray this in Jesus' Name. Amen.

KIDZ

When you wake up in the morning, do you feel like there is something important for you to accomplish that day?

You should! God said in Ephesians 2:10, "We are God's handiwork, created in Christ Jesus to do good works, which God prepared in advance for us to do" (NIV).

If you have a disability or challenges that make things more difficult than for other kids, I have good news for you!

God can use your weaknesses as well as your strengths. He has a good purpose for you each day. And don't forget, EVERYONE has both strengths and weaknesses, to some degree.

Talk to your mom or dad about some creative things you can do that are away from the TV, computer, and iPad! Try to do at least one creative activity each day (such as art, helping someone with a project, learning a new skill of any sort).

Here are some tips to help you have a day where you grow in new skills:

*Draw something and show someone you love.

*Write a kind note to someone, or ask your parent to help you write it.

*Help your mom make something yummy for your family to eat.

*Surprise your parents by doing something you are able to do. Maybe you are able to clean your room. Or maybe it is something else. But try every day to make someone you love happy.

*Next time someone says "hi" to you, look at them and smile. That's a little kindness that goes a long way.

*Ask your teacher or Sunday school teacher what you can do to help her/him.

These little things will give you a sense of purpose. And the more you do things like this, the more you will look for other meaningful things to do with your day.

TWO

I Need to Be Part of a Healthy Family

No [person] is an island, entire of itself; every [person] is a piece of the continent, a part of the main.

JOHN DONNE

John Donne was right. God has made us not to be an island, but to be part of the whole. Why? Because He desires that we touch each other's lives in a significant way and that each and every person show forth a facet of His own character. That is why deep down inside we all want to be part of the whole in some way—we were created like that! We are all relational creatures, and our kids who have special needs are no different. Romans 12:5, in speaking of how God designed His people to relate to one another, says, we are "individually members of one another," that is, we need each other!

The family is the perfect "boot camp" for learning how to fit in with all social contexts. It is, or at least should be, a safe place to learn, grow, and discover who we are. The young person who has special needs is especially dependent on family not only for support, but for "training" in social skills and in learning the art of being part of the whole.

When the Outside World Seems Wrong, Home Can Seem Right

It's a mad, bad, sad world out there sometimes. Kids who have special needs probably feel the intensity of that reality more than most as they are constantly feeling a little out of step with their peers, with the pace of life, with achievement expectations. It's hard to get knocked around in a world that travels too fast for you and where others rarely will slow down long enough to help you on your way. It can sometimes seem like the whole world is wrong for you when you have a disability or limitation that hinders you from keeping up.

Yes, the whole world can seem wrong, but how wonderful it is when home seems right!

Making the home a place of comfort involves a lot of things, and I'm sure you could share many of your own, but following are a few homey characteristics to think about:

People Who Are Glad to See You. There's nothing like being greeted by a smile! It's so simple, yet easy to forget. Did you know our faces are like a mirror to our kids? They look at our face to see who they are. When they look in this "mirror," do they see a scowl of disapproval or a smile of pleasure? Oh how a child with special challenges needs to see a smile of delight on the face of his parents! Home should be a place of smiles. I often walk by a mirror and am startled at what a scowl I have on my face! Scowls seem to come easily; smiles, on the other hand, need to be cultivated.

Traditions. Traditions are a symbol of the unique community that is your family. Sometimes kids with autism can get anxious because of a change in the normal schedule during holidays.

Brittany Fichter points out in her blog that having the same traditions each year can make a child who depends on structure feel safe and even enjoy and look forward to the holidays because of them.[1]

But traditions go way beyond the holidays. Jay Payleitner, author of *52 Things Kids Need from a Dad,* tells of how for years he bought marshmallow Peeps for his wife the minute they hit the shelf in the spring because she loves them so much. Now he doesn't have to buy them for her anymore. His kids buy them for her every year![2] Tradition makes for togetherness!

Creative Bible Studies. "My kids would never pay attention long enough to have a family Bible study." If that's what you're thinking, don't be so sure! Get out the old clothes, scarves, and make up, and have them dress up like the Bible characters of the story you want to study. Kids with significant limitations can participate by dressing up to represent a Bible character. He or she may not fully understand the message of the study, but will get this important message: I'm part of this family! Drama is something that sticks in a kid's mind, and suddenly, he is studying the Bible without even realizing it.

Older kids may not want to dress up, but might enjoy other kinds of fun visuals. Once our family was studying the book of James where it says, "Be quick to hear; slow to speak, and slow to anger" (1:19). So Dad volunteered to put a piece of duct tape over his mouth while the rest of us in the family gave him "constructive criticism," that is, ways he could improve. The tape, of course, kept him from defending himself and required him to just listen! The kids were beside themselves with the very fun time and Mike's being such a good sport helped us all to take in a Bible lesson we never forgot.

Meals Together. Following is a report found on theFamilyDinnerProject.org:

> *Over the past 15 years, research has shown what parents have known for a long time: Sharing a fun family meal is good for the spirit, brain and health of all family members.*[3]

This website also provides recipes, such as "one pot wonders," and conversation starters for kids and teens, such as "Do you know the story about how your parents met?" or "If you could be an animal, what would you want to be, and why?" Check out The Family Dinner Project. It's a great resource!

Our culture tends to make the home kind of a pit stop to quickly refuel, change clothes, and move on to the next activity. Even the life of a kid with special needs can come to have that flavor. But home was meant to be a place to linger awhile and build the kind of community that kids need.

Hospitality. It's often difficult for our kids who have a disability to get out socially, and many times they suffer the rejection of not being invited to friends' homes or to birthday parties. The solution? Make your home the "happenin' place" to be!

Once we had Brad's Sunday school class over for a pizza party after church. There were about thirty kids and they had a blast! Suddenly, our son was not left out. His peers stopped seeing him as the boy in the wheelchair when they got a chance to see him in his home environment.

The other advantage to "bringing the mountain to Mohammed," so to speak, is that in your home, you can direct the activities and so have the opportunity to select games and activities that your child can actually participate in.

First Peter 4:9 says, "Show hospitality to one another without grumbling" (ESV). I guess it's tempting to do a little grumbling at clean up time after having a houseful of kids! But hospitality is something that God will bless, and especially kids with challenges that make socializing difficult, will be helped by opening our homes to those who could be their friends.

It is an un-special need to have a welcoming home in which to relax, have fun, and feel part of a community.

Rules Make a Home More Homey

Rules? I'm kidding, right? Don't rules make a home rigid, un-homey, and stifling?

No, "rules" have gotten a bad rap in our society, kind of like good manners have. We've been conditioned to think of rules as harsh and burdensome, stifling the spirit, spoiling the fun. To make matters worse, we have often been led to believe that it is unfair to impose rules upon young people who have special needs.

But in any community, and family *is* a community, people have to agree on ways to live together and get along. That's all. Rules are not such an ominous concept when you think of them as tools for people who love each other to get along with each other and to be better equipped to live happily in the society of one another.

I have seen homes where the young person with special needs is the only child who is not accountable to follow family rules. The other children in the family may try to be understanding, but deep in their little hearts, they just may be thinking, "No fair!"

Your family needs for all its members to live by the same rules. I know, there are complications. But the same rules should apply with perhaps different applications to accommodate the unique bents and limitations of your child. Learning to live by the rules is vitally important, for there will be rules outside the home too; and remember, the home is boot camp!

Rules aren't all negative; in fact, if possible, they should be stated as positives. Take the principle above that families benefit by eating meals together. Your mealtime rules can be stated as positives. This helps kids know what to do, rather than always what not to do: *Use a voice that is pleasant to others. Keep hands and feet to yourself (this takes care of hitting, pinching, kicking). Listen when someone is talking and let them finish before you talk. Ask mom if you can help to clear the table rather than just getting up and leaving.* Stating rules in a positive way is better than a bunch of negatives. It tells kids what to do. Kids are full of energy, so they really respond better to directives that give them something to do with all that energy and oomph!

Don't be afraid of family rules! Only be afraid of rigid, inflexible rules that stifle. Good rules can bless your family with order and civility.

No One Is the Center in a Healthy Home

"I hated that my brother's needs came first and he got more attention than I did. I wish I had autism so you would play with ME for a change."[4]

Such was a comment from the sibling of a child whose parents obviously found it difficult to care for their son who had special needs while not being overwhelmed and consumed by it. I don't say that in a judgmental way; well do I know that there is a constant vortex-like pull which, if allowed to do so, will suck the entire family into a swirling and unending focus on special needs.

Gina Demillo Wagner wrote in her article "Having a Special Needs Brother Does Not Make Me Lucky," "Truth is, I grew up with the heavy weight of responsibility, not only to make up for every one of Alan's limitations, but to be wholly and completely un-needy. If he was the special-needs kid, I had to be no-needs."[5]

A young person with special issues or disabilities, like any other child, needs to know that he is welcome in his home and among his family members. Yet, there can be a tendency in a home to either marginalize the special child, so that he is not part of the main flow of the home, or just the opposite, and perhaps more often, to allow this young person and his needs to be the center of attention.

Here is what one mother said about how autism affected her family life: "The child with autism sucks up your physical, financial, and emotional resources, leaving little left for the rest of the family."[6]

One way to avoid spending an excessive amount of finances, time, and energy on our children's extra challenges is to be selective about therapies and interventions. Hans Hofmann, an expressionist painter, has said, "The ability to simplify means to eliminate the unnecessary so that the necessary may speak." As with paintings, so with life, and specifically with interventions for our kids. Too much can get crowded and burdensome, especially for the child. Choose the very best for your child, giving her the time and space to grow from it. And as an added benefit, the atmosphere of the home will be more relaxed.

Perhaps the most crucial step parents can take in keeping a balance in the home and thus preventing siblings from feeling resentful and parents from burning out is to be determined to discover at what level the special child is able to obey and comply with the family rules and to hold him or her accountable to it.

Often, there is a "she can't help it" feeling on the part of parents, and this lends itself to the child's needs, wants, and sometimes fits of anger, to disrupt the peaceful flow of the home.

So how do you know what the child is or is not capable of? Test it!

There are ways to find out what our children can really do. I remember a time when I wasn't sure what Brad was capable of physically. He was born when we lived in a two-story home, *and this mom was tired*! We were not in a financial position at that time to be able to move to a home more suitable for our situation. It was okay to lift him up the stairs when he was a baby, but as he grew, I really wanted him to get up the stairs on his own, if he could. I would put him down and ask him to crawl up, and he would just plop! Yet, I could feel that his muscles were stronger, and I felt that he had the potential to crawl up the stairs. I had laboriously and often placed his hands, then his knees on the stairs, giving him a feel for how it worked, and we would get up the stairs together. But when asked to try it himself—plop! Then a wry little grin would appear, making me wonder if he could do more than he was demonstrating.

He was about three years old at the time and had his sights on a yellow miner's hat at the toy store. I told him that if he would try very hard to get up the stairs by himself, the miner's hat was his! I thought it would be weeks, perhaps months, before he achieved such an out-of-reach goal. But wouldn't you know it, as soon as he heard of the prized hat, he slithered right up the stairs before my astonished eyes! And he did become the proud owner of a yellow miner's hat with a light on the front.

Although I didn't make him crawl up those stairs often, for

I knew it was difficult, I did expect him from that point on to get up the stairs by himself at times.

Yes, this made life easier for me, but I was not the one who benefited the most. I pushed my son to go beyond what he felt he wanted to do; and in the years to come, he was blessed both physically and emotionally by stretching his capabilities. At first it was obedience, but when he grew up, he literally thanked me for those times when I required more of him than he was comfortable with.

Even in cases where the child is not able to communicate or has cognitive limitations, there are ways to find out what our kids can and cannot do. We just have to keep our parent-radar sharp.

Do make obedience a goal, and please don't see this as a negative for your kids. God says obedience to parents is so that it will be well with them, so that their lives will be blessed. And there is even a promise that they could live longer by putting themselves under their parents' protective care (see Ephesians 6:1-2).

Think about it: Is it not true that your child will be much more likely to "fit in" both inside and outside of the home if she obeys your directives? Will she not gain self-control and become more aware of the feelings of others? Do her the favor of expecting obedience. It is your gift to your beloved son or daughter that will keep giving throughout their lives.

No one is the center in a healthy home. The family could be viewed as a group of people who love each other holding hands to form a circle. No one person is central, but everyone is important. Some may have greater needs than others, and that is taken into account, but everyone is part of the circle.

Your child has an un-special need to be an integral part of the family while not being the hub of the parents' time and energy, nor of the family itself.

Everyone Is a Welcome Member in a Healthy Home

Ohana means family.
Family means nobody gets left behind...
—Lilo and Stitch

In that circle, which is family, there may be those who move slower, need more care, or in some cases, are just plain harder to live with. But the circle can still stay intact, no member losing the grip of the hand of his family members. Granted, this is not always easy. Saying that the special child needs to be a welcome member doesn't mean that he will participate in exactly the same way that his siblings might.

I tried hard to make our home life "normal." But so often it just didn't work. I suppose I had in my mind that in order for my son to be a welcome member of the family, he had to participate in typical ways, but it didn't take long to realize that often this was not possible.

I remember one time I decided that I would take Ricky and Brad swimming. I knew it wouldn't work at the big pool with all the splashing and commotion, so we went to a local hotel that had a pool. I was so excited that we could enjoy an event together doing something that other people did. We got in, and Brad swallowed water and threw up in the pool. Then, of course, in the locker room, I had the usual impossible time getting him dressed because there was only a skinny bench and a cement floor to lay him on. Our event, which we were all so excited about, ended up in mom holding back her tears.

After some time of trying, I finally had to give in to the fact that Brad would not be able to do many of the things that his brother did. I had to come to grips with the reality that no matter how much I wanted my son to have completely typical participation in our family, he really never would.

Having said that, however, I will have to add that as I look at photo albums, I see my boys lying in a tent, punching each other (great fun for boys); sitting in a bubble bath, splashing each other when they were very young; lounging in an over-stuffed chair, looking at picture books together; each spraying his brother with a garden hose in the backyard; leaning against a headboard, each with a parakeet on his shoulder and a cat on his lap (Yep! The birds and the cat got along famously.). I see them on a boat wearing life jackets, making "yuk" faces while worming the hook. Then there were the mom-directed activities such as when the two hermit crabs would "race" from the center of a hula hoop. Brad could cheer with the rest of the kids who had gathered for the fun.

So although the boys couldn't go out and throw a ball or run around the neighborhood, they did find ways to relate in their brother-type way. Their barriers were not only physical as Ricky's thought processes went at lightning speed, and Brad's were much slower (which wasn't always a bad thing!). But they were able to overcome that too by relating in their creative ways. Ricky was often great at adapting to his brother's style.

Whatever it takes, and whatever accommodations need to be made, the important thing is to include your son or daughter in the general flow of the family. We as parents may feel the pain of "what could have been," but the child will feel welcome and satisfied if he or she is part of things, even if it is not in the typical way or in the way that other families do things. We often think our child is responding to disappointments as we are, when really what matters to him most is that he is included and accepted for who he is.

Laughter Is the Best Medicine

When I was a little girl, I used to read my mom's *Reader's Digest*, and I still recall the section entitled "Laughter Is the Best Medicine." Little did I know how much that little piece of wisdom would become a lifeline for me later on!

Charles Dickens said, "There is nothing in the world so irresistibly contagious as laughter and good humor." Try with all your might to have times when you and your family members are able to put it all aside and be lighthearted. Show them by your example that although the problems are real, they don't have to consume the persons or the family. After all, the apostle Paul was a prisoner in a Roman jail when he wrote, "Rejoice in the Lord always; again I will say, rejoice!" (Philippians 4:4).

When you laugh with someone, you form an instant and often inseparable bond. The family who laughs often will be a family in which the members are more resistant to bitterness and anger. It will create a closeness and a desire to spend more time together. Laugh and enjoy those moments that God gives when we can put the burdens aside for just a while and enjoy each other's company!

Show Me What It Looks Like to Love

According to many articles, there are "statistics" that say the divorce rate for parents who have kids with special needs is 80 percent. Turns out, there is no evidence for those statistics. However, we all know, statistics or no statistics, what a strain it can be on a marriage when daily special needs are introduced into the family.

Still, let's begin with an ideal situation. I am well aware that very few marriage relationships are ideal. As my pastor often says, "We are messy people," meaning, in a variety of ways, our lives are not ideal! But there is value in looking at the ideal situation. Zig Ziglar has said, "If you aim at nothing, you will hit it every time!" But if we look at marriage as it could be, we may get our arrow just a little closer to the ideal.

Ideally, a marriage relationship in a home is a picture to the children who live in that home of what love looks like. Josh McDowell has said, "We do not develop habits of genuine love automatically. We learn by watching effective role models— most specifically by observing how our parents express love for each other day in and day out."

Though the strain is great, the man and woman who fell in love and married each other should not allow the pressures associated with difficult child issues to come between them. Their relationship is first. The children benefit from mom and dad holding on tenaciously to their priority relationship because it is actually just as, if not more, important to them that mom and dad love each other as it is that mom and dad love them! It is a fact that children, typical children and children with special needs, benefit much more from seeing that mom and dad are enjoying a committed and loving relationship than they benefit from any amount of piano lessons, soccer involvement, or for the special child, therapies! No amount of money or attention toward the kids can make up for the need they have in their souls to see that mom and dad are doing well together. It brings a kind of health and stability that little else in this world can bring.

Okay, there is the ideal, and although it may seem out of reach in light of the pressures associated with raising children, and especially children with difficult challenges, I believe every word of the ideal is true.

So now what about what is for most of us, real life? The "messy" part? I mentioned my pastor talks about us being messy people, but he adds that as we seek God's help, we can nevertheless be ever moving in a more positive direction.

One thing a couple can do is connect without the kids once a week. Amy Baskin, author of *More Than a Mom*, said,

> *Some couples say they can't go out. Could it be they've forgotten how to be a couple? You need to relearn this. Schedule in a weekly date. Nurture the part of your relationship that's outside of parenting.*
>
> *What if your child's needs are so involved that you can't leave them? Plan and schedule in-home dates. With creativity, there's no reason you can't date your partner.*[7]

Then there's a post, the author identified only by "Professor," on *The Thinking Mom's Revolution*. It is written by a mom who at the time of the writing of the post was separated from her spouse because of the pressures of raising a child with special needs. Still she wishes they had made time for each other.

> *I've noticed that there's one area that gets shafted for almost all special-needs parents: "together time," also known as "date night." Burnt-out folks find it difficult to plan fun activities for themselves and their partner. Spending money on it can also be difficult when you're balancing it against this week's organic food or speech therapy. But doesn't it seem that marriages where the relationship is a top priority are more fun and resilient? Chalk that up to another lesson learned.*[8]

What's the big deal about date night? I think it has to do with the words of a song I heard a long time ago, "I think you'd take my hand if you would understand the way I feel..." When a husband and wife get alone, they have an opportunity to share their feelings about things, and just maybe that will cause understanding and break down barriers. Sure, the sharing of feelings may not come to the surface for a while, but when they do, healing can begin to take place.

His Compassions Are New Every Morning

The LORD's lovingkindnesses indeed never cease,
For His compassions never fail,
They are new every morning;
Great is your faithfulness.
Lamentations 3:22-23

God's mercies are new every morning, so says the prophet Jeremiah, and because of that, we can take our family situation, whatever it may be, and ask God to help us to make it a healthy environment where kids learn what love looks like. Shoot for the ideal, but if the arrow misses that mark, know that we have a gracious God who is for us and for our family, and who will honor our seeking Him and desiring to move forward in a positive direction from wherever we might find ourselves.

Adrian Rogers said this: "The same Jesus who turned water into wine can transform your home, your family, and your future. He is still in the miracle-working business, and His business is the business of transformation."

Time to Soar

* *Explore ways to help your kids understand their sibling who has special needs.*

I recently looked through a book written by a 14 year old young man named Daniel Stefanski, who has autism, entitled: *How to Talk to an Autistic Kid*. In it, he says, "Even though my brain is different, I'm still a kid. I like to have fun and I want to have friends."[9] How often kids are misunderstood, and perhaps, particularly kids who have different needs than others do. Just having siblings read a book like this can help them to have some "aha" moments concerning their sibling who has special needs.

Not all areas of special needs are so fortunate to have the amount of growing information there is available to help understand autism, but no matter what form the special need takes, the principle is the same: Do everything as a parent possible to understand it and it's ramifications, and help your other children to do the same with their special sibling.

And don't forget! Help the child who has special needs to also understand the needs of his or her parents and siblings as well. It has to work both ways and in all directions of the family dynamic in order for the family to be all that God created it to be.

Read Ephesians 6:1-2 to your children:

Children obey your parents in the Lord, for this is right. Honor your father and your mother (which is the first commandment with a promise), so that it may be well with you, and that you may live long on the earth.

Explain that God has given this command to bless them! Ask them questions concerning how they feel about obeying mom and dad. Pray out loud with them, asking God to make you and your spouse good and fair parents, and asking God to make the children to be happy in their obedience to their parents.

*If you have not already, begin to see rules in your home as a positive.

Here's a possible exercise to do with your kids: Ask them to verbalize or write down all the ways they can think of that rules in the home make life better for everyone. If they can't think of any, help them out! This exercise is to help them see that rules are not just to make parents have an easier life, but rather to make all family members have a better home life!

*Laugh!

It can be as simple as watching a funny, clean movie together that everyone will enjoy. Eat popcorn. Laugh together some- time this week. Last Thanksgiving our family had three gen- erations together, and we watched *Mr. Magoo*. My mom said afterward, "I feel so good inside. I had forgotten what it feels like to laugh!"

KIDZ

Your family deserves your very best...they are your family! Yet sometimes we give our families our very worst behavior. We complain; we whine and cry; we don't use any manners around them. But home should be a place where all family members can relax and find encouragement from each other.

That's why your parents make family rules. Rules are so that everyone can live together peacefully. Home should be where everyone feels respected and loved. Even table manners are about respect. Here's a poem written by a man a long time ago describing Goops. What are Goops? They are people (in the poet's imagination) who aren't thinking about the other people who are at the table with them:

> The Goops they lick their fingers,
> And the Goops they lick their knives;
> They spill their broth on the tablecloth—
> O, they lead disgusting lives!
> The Goops they talk while eating,
> And loud and fast they chew;
> And that is why I'm glad that I
> Am not a Goop—are you?
> Gelett Burgess, 1900[10]

Don't be a Goop! Don't cry and complain when your family members are trying to have a peaceful meal. Why should one person ruin the whole family's mealtime?

And manners aren't just at mealtime. Manners are always. Manners say, "You are important and so I am going to take responsibility for my behavior so that you feel respected."

Manners teach you to be "a giver." You might say, "Well, I have nothing to give." But you are wrong! You can give a smile; you can give a kind word or look; you can give your family a lot of things that seem small, but are really big deals...because they make someone feel loved and respected. Not only that, but when you learn to give these little gestures of good manners to your family, you will also learn to give them to others outside your family, and that will likely make people like you and want to be around you! Family is like a "boot camp." It is where you learn how to live and to love!

THREE

I Need a Personal Faith in God

Joy is a by-product not of happy circumstances,
education, or talent,
but of a healthy relationship with God
and a determination to love Him no matter what.

BARBARA JOHNSON

For I am convinced that...[no] created thing
will be able to separate us from the love of God,
which is in Christ Jesus our Lord.

Romans 8:38-39

What does faith look like in the average special-needs family? I think I can guess. Perhaps it looks like going to church and feeling exhausted by lunchtime from the struggle of knowing your child is having a hard time fitting in at his Sunday school class. There's likely a feeling of trying to resign to the fact that your family will always feel somewhat isolated in their situation, kind of a sinking feeling in the pit of your stomach that other families have a much simpler and, perhaps you wonder, a more blessed life. You go to the service and sing of the God of mercy and love, and you wouldn't admit it, perhaps not even to yourself, that what you see in front of your eyes daily—the shriveled limbs, the struggling mind, the seeming uncontrollable impulses of your child—keep interrupting the words of the songs with, "Really?" There seems to be a contradiction between what is being proclaimed at church in word and song, and the reality of your life.

Then there's the rest of the week, the six other days. Prayer is perhaps reduced to "Help, Lord!" And this God of love has a hard time finding a place in the constant stress and hyper-emotion of knowing that your child is not, and perhaps never will be, the healthy and whole person you hoped he or she would be.

Is there room for faith in God in this scene...a personal and active faith that transcends the challenges and brings a sense of peace and joy to the heart and home?

I can relate to every issue suggested above, and this chapter isn't going to "fix" the inevitable stress and occasional doubting of God's love that occur when a child has serious issues. But I'd like to offer some hope, some truth, some realities about gaining a perspective that can keep your eyes "on the things above" (Colossians 3:2) and that can help both you and your children to experience the joy of living in a world of faith. Still, life is hard...

Hard Doesn't Mean Bad

A friend of mine confided in me while we were having a conversation over lunch, "Life is hard." In my mind I contrasted that to the bumper sticker I often see "Life is good."

Are these two different perspectives, one from a pessimist, the other from an optimist? After thinking about my own view of life, I have concluded that life is hard, *and* life is good!

Hard doesn't mean bad. Hard just means hard, and so often good things come from the hardest experiences in life. Having said that, I have to admit that sometimes I have thought of Tevye's comment to God in *Fiddler on the Roof*, "I know, I know, we are the chosen people. But once in a while, couldn't You choose someone else?"

God's blessings in the form of trials are often hazy when we are overwhelmed by the difficulty of it all. And if you're like me, sometimes you wish that if blessings come from adversity, that God would bless someone else!

Yet as Christians, deep down inside we know it is true: "God causes all things to work together for good to those who love God" (Romans 8:28)... familiar to many of us, but the truth of it never wears out.

Someone has said, "Every time you find humor in a difficult situation, you win." And I would add: Every time you find some form of good in a difficult situation, you win...for choosing to find good when life is hard is evidence of faith in the God who promises that all things work together for good to those who love Him and who are called to His purpose.

Often the ultimate good doesn't show up for a while and we are able to recognize it only in retrospect. Philip Yancey said in his book *Disappointment with God*, "Faith means believing in advance what will only make sense in reverse."[1] Yet all along the way, there are glimpses of good and of blessing in the hardest of times.

I got the following note last Christmas from my friend Ange, who lives in Zimbabwe and whose daughter Amy had at that time been in a hospital in South Africa for over a month. I love the last line, for it is living proof that "some form of good" can be found in any situation.

*Amy managed 5 minutes on pressure support
ventilation today. Wow this looks like a long road. Most
of the teams normally involved (except the doctors) are
on Christmas holiday & we feel a little shelved till new
year. Hard because we are supposed to be going back
to Zimbabwe on 1 Jan., Gords to work, Josie & Faith to
school. We had hoped to be out of ICU by Christmas.
On a positive note, Gorden & I had supper together in
the hospital foyer for the first time in ages. We'll find
romance anywhere! :)*

Then, I got another note when this family got home a couple
of months later:

*Amy had a tracheostomy early December when she was
in a critical state, supposedly as a temporary measure
but now they believe it's permanent In answer to your
question, yes she can talk and eat now, and we change
the trachy every day. I was terribly sad at first because I
thought I'd never again hear her sing, but she blocks the
hole (in her throat) and sings at the top of her voice!*

Amy has learned from her parents' faith, for it takes faith to
find romance in a hospital foyer, and it takes faith to sing at the
top of one's voice when you have a respirator tube to deal with.
When the hard things are set against the reality that there is a
loving, good, and sovereign God personally involved in every
detail of one's life, there is amazing evidence that the human
spirit cannot be squelched by adversity. This is part of the good
that can come from hard times—realizing that our spirit is
more resilient than we could have imagined.

Yet, it's not that simple. Adversity and daily stress can

plunge both adults and children into depression, anxiety, and a feeling of hopelessness. And when that happens, hard really does mean bad for that moment!

But there is a refuge for those who will know that God's Word is more than sermon material, it is our very life. Jesus said, "Man shall not live on bread alone, but on every word that proceeds out of the mouth of God" (Matthew 4:4).

So I asked Ange to share how she and her husband Gorden have made God's Word to be a fortress and strength to their family in a practical way. Here is what she shared:

There were two ways in which I felt God met us as a Rock, in our family. One was in the Scriptures we memorised. It was like He presented us with Scriptures beforehand which were just what we needed for the crisis time. Josie had been learning Eph 6:10-18 at school, so we learned it as a family, and it was so relevant. Amy had learned Ps 23. The one thing she was afraid of was not the operation, or pain afterwards, or what might happen, but the time of being put to sleep, the anesthesia. She said it was like opening a bag of sharks. So when they wheeled her into (the operating room) she started saying Ps 23 through her tears, and fell asleep part-way through. We learned Zeph 3:17 with dramatic actions, and when my heart broke at saying goodbye to the little ones for another month, I kept reminding them and myself of it—God doing for them all the things I wished I could do—delighting in them, quieting them, rejoicing over and with them. Scripture became very real for us and proved to be a solid Rock. Recently I heard Josie remark that she was upset so she

was going to read the Bible. What an eternal treasure
for her, to know she can find strength in the Word!

The second way was in relinquishing. During Amy's
worst times we felt compelled to relinquish her to God,
pray for His will to be done and entrust her to Him, not
presuming what His will might be but knowing she was
eternally safe. It was a constant choice, and again to
relinquish Josie and Faith knowing the parting would
be hard, but somehow when we relinquished our most
precious children to Him, His power was released to
work in their hearts. And God's presence and love filled
us all with peace and strength.

I know that both Ange and ten-year-old Amy have been
"down in the dumps" at different times; who wouldn't be in
their situation? But I think of Proverbs 24:16, "A righteous
[person] falls seven times, and rises again." The word *righteous*
doesn't mean perfect; it means someone who is trusting in God;
and "seven times" isn't meant to be a number to be counted, but
means "many times" or "repeatedly."

No, the human spirit cannot be ultimately squelched, when the
Creator is invited to be at home in that spirit. Having that kind of
relationship with God is an un-special need.

When You Feel Too Weak to Encourage Your Child

How do you tell a young person who is distressed in an ongoing way of a loving, wise, and compassionate God? How do
you believe it yourself when what you see in front of your eyes
contradicts it all—a limited body, a struggling mind, a puzzling
condition that brings continual frustration and sorrow? How

do you encourage a child to faith when your own faith is wavering and you feel so weak?

Here's what I used to say to my teenage son Brad: "Bradley, I don't know if I could handle your disability as well as you do...in fact, I'm quite sure that I couldn't. And I don't know why God has allowed this in your life. But in spite of my own limitations of understanding, I'm going to tell you the truth from God's Word, that He loves you, that He has a good plan for your life, and that you will someday be grateful for everything He has given when you see Him face to face. This is all I know, Brad. As your parent, I need to tell you the truth, even if I myself have a hard time understanding it, and sometimes even believing it. But let's believe God's Word together, and seek His joy." Often I would remember the words of Ney Bailey who wrote *Faith Is Not a Feeling*, "God's Word is truer than anything we feel. God's Word is truer than any circumstance we have."

In most cases, we can't change our child's situation, but we can encourage him to gain a perspective that helps him to live on a higher plane than his circumstances.

Remember what God says about His word in Isaiah 55:10-11:

> *For as the rain and the snow come down from heaven,*
> *and do not return there without watering the earth and*
> *making it bear and sprout, and furnishing seed to the*
> *sower and bread to the eater; so will My word be which*
> *goes forth from My mouth; it will not return to Me*
> *empty, without accomplishing what I desire, and with-*
> *out succeeding in the matter for which I sent it.*

You don't have to be a super-Christian in order to help your son or daughter. You can share with her your own doubts and struggles, but always speak to her of truth. God's Word does not return to Him without accomplishing good things: fruit, life, joy, and strength. *You as the parent don't have to be a perfect example of faith; simply join your child in the faith journey and set God's Word before your family.*

It's a positive for your kids to know that you have doubts, fears, and weaknesses. How will they really know how to deal with their own if they think that these emotions and soul conditions are not part of the Christian life? They are indeed part of the Christian life, and our kids look to us to know how to handle them.

It is an un-special need to have a role model of consistent, albeit sometimes struggling, faith.

The Power of Listening

Recently, Mike and I attended a memorial service that changed our lives. We didn't even know this person. His name was Jan, a younger man who died of cancer. We only went because we knew his sister and wanted to be supportive of her. Little did we know how Jan's life would touch our own!

The sharing time came and thus started the most amazing accounts of a person touching people's lives, and it all revolved around Jan's giftedness to listen! There were homeless people, neighbors, couples whose marriages were in trouble, there were old people and young people—they all were moved by Jan's listening heart and gave testimony to his effect on their situations. One friend of Jan's felt compelled to go up to the stairs of the church and demonstrate how Jan would listen: "He would hunker down and get comfortable, like this. Then he would set his gaze on me, and say, 'What's going on with you, brother?'

James 1:19 says, "Be quick to hear, slow to speak." There

is power in active, intentional, and respectful listening. The description of Jan from those whose lives he touched was the perfect picture of James 1:19 because Jan would be quick and deliberate in his "hearing" and then he would slowly share the truth of God's Word, which found fertile soil in the hearts of these individuals who felt so valued.

Have you ever had someone listen to you? I mean really "hunker down" and set their gaze on you and communicate through body language that what is in your soul matters to them? When that happens, life suddenly doesn't seem so bad. And you are much more open to whatever that person wants to share with you.

Kids are no different. Our kids with special needs are especially hungry to have someone care about what is inside of their soul, for it's something they likely don't experience very often. Their young hearts will respond to respectful attentiveness, and that will set the stage for you to tell them about the love of God.

Imparting faith to children involves listening to them, for that is the beginning of giving them an understanding of their value before God. It is an un-special need to be valued enough to be listened to attentively.

Listening is the opposite of lecturing. All parents could write a book entitled *If I Knew Then What I Know Now* when they get to the end of the parenting years. My book would have this theme: To lecture less and to listen more!

Josh McDowell has said, "Part of good communication is listening with the eyes as well as with the ears." Our culture moves so fast. As a special parent you are probably moving from therapy session to school meeting to doctor appointment, but nothing will touch the life of your precious child more than slowing down and listening to his words and to his heart. You might have a child who is nonverbal, but you can still "listen" by giving him or her your undivided attention in a quiet setting.

Heaven

Then the eyes of the blind will be opened
And the ears of the deaf will be unstopped.
Then the lame will leap like a deer,
And the tongue of the mute will shout for joy.
Isaiah 35:5-6

These words in the book of Isaiah can send chills down your spine if they are taken seriously! Think about it, those who know Christ will see their loved ones who have lived with disability on earth run and leap and shout for joy, with perfect bodies and clear minds such as none of us has ever experienced! (And has it ever occurred to you that by far, most of us will end up with disabilities of some sort by the time we reach old age?)

Joni Eareckson Tada has said, "I can still hardly believe it. I, with shriveled, bent fingers, atrophied muscles, gnarled knees, and no feeling from the shoulders down, will one day have a new body—light, bright, and clothed in righteousness—powerful and dazzling."[2]

It would be incomplete, to say the least, to have a chapter on faith without mentioning the reality of our hope of heaven.

Instilling faith in kids is not a religious practice; rather it is showing them by example how to be grounded in the hope that Hebrews 6:19 says is "an anchor of the soul." It shouldn't be a burden to do this, rather a burden-lifter, for faith, especially faith in heaven, provides a solid anchor in our souls to give us stability and joy during the storms of life that we encounter. Max Lucado prayed, "Teach us to set our hopes on heaven, to hold firmly to the promise of eternal life, so that we can withstand the struggles and storms of this world."

If you have kids with limitations, try to imagine them as they will be—perfect in mind and body, completely able, beautiful, and whole. Take the opportunity to tell them what they have to look forward to as believers in Christ. They, too, can have a new perspective in realizing that we who know Jesus are literally "just passin' through." Peter talks about our "stay" upon the earth, and that we are strangers and aliens here (1 Peter 1:17; 2:11). Don't worry that you are being "pie in the sky" if you set your hope on heaven and encourage your kids to do the same. C.S. Lewis said, "Aim at Heaven, and you will get Earth 'thrown in'; aim at Earth and you will get neither."[3]

I have felt a bit like a split personality since I have been bereaved now of two beloved children. One minute, I am crying and grieving because of our loss; the next, I seem to get a realization of the reality of joy that my children are experiencing, and I am about to burst with happiness. I remember one day shortly after Brad left us, I turned on some music (loud) and danced my heart out in the living room, because my joy could not be contained! Does that seem like strange behavior? Well, I'm in good company; David danced before the Lord with all his might (2 Samuel 6:14), and Psalm 149:3 says, "Let them praise His name with dancing; let them sing praises to Him with timbrel and lyre." (Can you imagine the dancing for joy that will go on in heaven?)

Have you noticed as a parent, perhaps especially as a mom, that if your kids are happy, you're happy? That's what I am experiencing. When I grasp truths such as "in your presence is fullness of joy" (Psalm 16:11) and "a day in Your courts is better than a thousand outside" (Psalm 84:10), how can I feel anything but happy? Yes, we can feel grief and joy at the same time. I suppose that is what Paul meant when he said we are not to grieve as those who have no hope (1 Thessalonians 4:13).

Heaven is our ultimate goal and what we and our children long for deep in our hearts, though we may not even realize it. In the last paragraphs of *The Last Battle,* C.S. Lewis wrote:

> *All their life in this world and all their adventures in Narnia had only been the cover and the title page; now at last they were beginning Chapter One of the Great Story, which no one on earth has read; which goes on forever; in which every chapter is better than the one before.*[4]

Time to Soar

Share truth with your child even when you feel weak in your own faith.

Think of how Ange and Gorden prepared their children for a very difficult time by memorizing Scripture. When you don't have anything to offer your kids in terms of faith, God's Word does! Take the opportunity to share your own doubts and fears, yet always point to the truth of God's Word. Memorize it together as a family, if possible. Remember the promise in Isaiah 55: God's word will never return to Him without accomplishing His purpose in the lives of those who receive it.

*Listen!

Granted, some young people will chatter your head off if they are given unrestrained attention in listening. So it's not that we listen completely attentively at all times. If we did, in some cases, we would be able to do little else! Rather, it's that we make times during the day when we are occupied with nothing but listening to the heart and soul of our child.

Make sure there is time alone with each child individually, and listen. Listening involves not speaking until your son or daughter has finished a complete thought. It involves body language that communicates, "I'm focused on you and you alone at this moment." Ditch the cell phone for a while.

A practice that I've been working on personally is if there is a thought shared that is disagreeable to me, I've been trying to ask a question rather than making a contradictory remark.

If the child is nonverbal, cognitively limited, or hyperactive and has a difficult time communicating thoughts that are easily understood, listen with your eyes more than your ears. Just let her know that you desire to understand her.

*Teach your kids about heaven.

Talk about heaven.

I personally stay away from testimonies of those who have gone to heaven and come back to tell about it. Although these accounts may or may not be valid, remember that God's Word is our only truly solid source of information.

Anne Graham Lotz wrote a charming book entitled: *Heaven, God's Promise for Me.* The book is full of beautiful illustrations, and in fact is a poem, but it is packed full of biblical truth about heaven.

Anne is Billy Graham and Ruth Bell Graham's daughter, and she emphasizes in the introduction of the book how her parents were intentional about teaching her and her siblings the truth of God. That is what we need to be: intentional—as well as vulnerable and having listening ears. *Then our kids will be on their way to having the most important un-special need of all met—the need to have a personal faith in God.*

KIDZ

God loves you. You've probably heard that before, but do you believe it? Does it matter in your life in a practical way?

At our house, there used to be a book around that had the title *If God Loves Me, Why Can't I Get My Locker Open?* I always liked that title because I picture a young person trying to get his or her school locker open and bringing God's love right down to the point of a real-life frustration!

And you may have sometimes had a secret question in your mind, "If God loves me so much, why is my life so hard? I mean, my life seems harder than other kids'. Maybe God loves them better."

That's actually a great question. Lots of kids and adults have that same question. Isn't God supposed to be able to do anything? Then why does He allow my life to be so hard?

One of the points your parents read in this chapter is that "hard doesn't mean bad." If God has allowed you to have a hard life, it isn't because He wants you to have a bad life!

We don't know why God allows some people to have more difficult lives than others, but we do know that He wants everyone to have a good life. This may be confusing to try to understand, but sometimes the hard things in our lives are the very things that can make our lives good.

Huh? What does that mean, and how can hard things be good?

Let me tell you a true story:

When Bethany Hamilton was a teenager, she had a really hard thing happen. While she was surfing in the ocean, a shark bit off her arm with one bite and, at the same time, took a bite out of her surfboard!

Bethany never had a disability before that. She was used to doing whatever she wanted, but now, she only has one arm. Here are some of the things she has said about her experience:

"I would never take my arm back if I could. What happened to me gives so much hope to people. God has a plan for each of you, and He loves you with all His heart."

Bethany's favorite verse is Jeremiah 29:11, "I know the plans I have for you, declares the LORD, plans for welfare (good) and not for evil, to give you a future and a hope" (ESV).

Bethany has chosen to turn a hard thing into a good thing, because she knows that her hard circumstance makes her more able to encourage others who also have hard circumstances. She said, "It's been amazing to touch people's lives!"

God can use your hard circumstances too! Talk to your mom or dad about ways that the hard things in your life could be used by God to encourage others. For example, if you have a positive attitude about your difficulties, maybe someone would think to themselves, "If that person has a positive attitude and faith in God, maybe I can too!"

FOUR

I Need to Be a Friend

If you go looking for a friend,
you're going to find they are scarce.
If you go out to be a friend, you'll find them everywhere.
Zig Ziglar

The only way to have a friend is to be one.
Ralph Waldo Emerson

Give, and it will be given to you.
Jesus, Luke 6:38

In order to put myself in the "shoes" of someone who has a significant disability, I have tried to imagine what I would feel if I were in a car accident, suddenly finding myself with a major disability and unable to do the things that formerly came to me with great ease. I imagine what kind of response I would desire from the friends and family who visited and cared for me. Would I want them to coddle me and say, "Oh you poor dear. We will take care of your every need." No, that would make me utterly depressed! I think I would long to hear a friend say, "Bev, you can't do some of the things you used to do, but there are plenty of things you *can* do. I would like to help you realize the gifts and abilities you have in your new situation, and encourage you to use them!" The coddling friends would be demonstrating pity. The friend I described would be honoring me with respect.

Our kids are no different. They want friends, real friends—friends who respect them, not pity them. It's difficult to communicate to teachers, other parents, and the kids who are your child's peers exactly what is going on; perhaps from their perspective, your child does have friends because others are "nice" to him. But what they don't realize is that there is a difference between respect and pity. Respect is what real friendship is about. Pity may look good from the outside, but in reality, it is the worst experience that can happen to a human being. It shrivels the soul and shreds all motivation to live life to the fullest.

We can start our son or daughter on a good path when we refuse to pity them, and when we give them social tools to make it less likely that others feel sorry for them, resulting in either rejection or pity. In providing these tools, we help to make it more likely that they will glean the respect of those around them.

My experience with this heartbreaking reality of my kids wanting friends was that I had to come to grips with the fact that no matter what I did or tried to do, I couldn't make people be friends with my kids! Young people are on the move. It is very rare when they are willing to slow down and give time to a relationship that hinders their social life.

But there is good news. We can't make people be friends with our kids, but we can give our sons and daughters the life skills they need to *be* a friend. There are no promised magic results, but for the young person who has issues that make friendship difficult, learning to be a friend is the most surefire way to move from being ignored or pitied, to being respected and, at least on some level, included.

On occasion, before writing on a subject, I will "google" the topic to see what others have to say. So I googled things such as "special-needs kids making friends." To my amazement, although there are an enormous amount of articles, books, and discussions on encouraging kids, teachers, and other parents to learn to be a friend to a special-needs child, I did not see one word written on helping the child who actually has the special needs to learn to be a friend to others! *This sets the stage for the pity-based relationship as opposed to the respect-based relationship.*

So what are some practical ways, some tools, we can impart to our kids that will help them learn to *be* a friend. Some of these tools have to do with changing our own attitudes; some have to do with simply analyzing what good friendships are made of.

It is an un-special need to be respected and to have friendships that involve mutual respect. It is an un-special need not only to have friends, but to be a friend.

Helping Kids to Know How to Be Givers

From the time we humans are born, there is no need to teach us to be takers—that comes naturally! But it takes a lifetime to learn to be a giver. Children may amaze and delight us at times by their acts of generosity. But learning to be a consistent and joyful giver is something that must be cultivated, and is what solid friendships are made of.

Although it is a lifelong journey involving effort for anyone to learn to be a consistent giver, kids with special needs have an especially difficult challenge in this. For one thing, I think of the times I have not been well in one way or another; maybe I was sick in bed, or I had an injury. It was difficult to think of anything or anyone but myself and my affliction during that time. Kids with disabilities are constantly struggling with their limitations, and so looking outward, I believe, is more difficult for them, just as for any of us when we are dealing with an unusual challenge. Still, because we love our children, we give them a lifelong gift when we encourage and help them to be others-aware, to look outward, and to be a giver.

Sean Barron, who coauthored the book *The Unwritten Rules of Social Relationships*, shares in detail within this book of his journey, his struggle, and his victories in learning to look outward and to be a giver in a social context.

Sean has been autistic from an early age. Sometimes we have the mistaken idea that all kids with autism are not interested in friendships or close relationships; however, most often, that just is not true. We mistake their behavior that is hard for us to understand for a lack of interest in friendship. Sean wrote, "I was desperate to have friends, to have people like me and admire me, and to be like everyone else."[1]

But being autistic, Sean lacked the innate social sense that most young people naturally possess, and so his efforts in friendship failed miserably. In fact, his thinking was so skewed that when a few of his classmates reached out to him, he told them, "Quit bothering me or I'll call the police," because he had so firmly in his mind that "no one likes Sean Barron."[2]

Sean's parents were stellar examples of persistence and excellence in communication with their son, staying up late at night with him in his teens for "talk therapy," which he said greatly helped his social understanding. Still, he never really came to grips with his autism until he watched a TV movie entitled *Son-Rise*. For some reason, it was that movie that made it clear to him that he had autism, what autism really was, and most importantly, that he could choose to overcome its weaknesses, at least to some degree. He said, "I understood for the first time that I was capable of working to become the person that I wanted to be." And again, "I started to turn my gaze outward; my world became more than myself."[3] With that goal, to turn his focus away from himself and onto others, Sean began the adventure of *being a friend*, rather than trying to make others like and admire him. He gained the respect of many others rather than pity or disdain from that point on.

Sean began to grow in awareness of some important stepping-stones toward enjoying healthy relationships, including, that he was responsible for his own behavior, no matter what others did or did not do. He also grew in his ability to ask questions, to let the other person talk, and to really listen to what they were saying, responding with empathetic replies. He found that simple questions like "So what's going on in your life?" were the key to being a friend, which was also the road to having true, meaningful, and respect-based friendships. Sean learned with determination to be "a giver" in conversation by listening. (Note: It was not the movie *Son-Rise* that brought Sean to these areas of awareness, but the movie simply touched a chord in him that began a process. The impetus for striking that chord will be different for different individuals.)

A Phantom World

"A phantom living in a world that was no world."[4] That's how Helen Keller, being both blind and deaf, described her existence before the arrival of teacher Anne Sullivan. This phantom world of hers was both dark and silent, and certainly did not, in fact at that time, could not, involve an awareness of the thoughts and feelings of others.

How did Helen's teacher help her to escape from the phantom world which held her captive? She did many things: She taught her to communicate; she taught her about the wonders of nature; but perhaps most significantly, she taught her "otherness," or being "others-aware." No matter what form a disability may take, this is the key to being released from a world of isolation—to be aware of the needs, the joys and sadnesses, and the desires of others.

One of the first things Anne undertook with Helen was to insist that her pupil use a utensil to eat, rather than wandering around eating off others' plates, which made especially visitors feel uncomfortable. This was the first step in Helen getting a grasp that in order to have positive relationships and escape her phantom world, she must understand how her actions affected others' feelings toward her. Prior to this, Helen's parents were willing to give in "for the sake of peace," but that only resulted in some friends and relatives advising them to put Helen in an institution since it was impossible for her to have "pleasant" relationships. Her brother James is depicted in *The Miracle Worker* as saying, "You really ought to put that child away...it is not pleasant to see her about.[5]" But Anne saw potential that others couldn't see. She knew that Helen's disability did not mean that she couldn't grow in her ability to feel compassion and respect toward others.

Your child may seem a million miles from being able to relate to other individuals in a giving way. But don't give up. It didn't come easily for Anne Sullivan either. That is why she said, "People seldom see the halting and painful steps by which the most insignificant success is achieved."

God has told us to "love one another with brotherly affection. Outdo one another in showing honor (respect)" (Romans 12:10, ESV). We may not fully understand the mystery of how much individuals with difficult conditions are capable of demonstrating love and respect to others, but we do know this: God has wired us all basically alike in our souls, and He has made us to be happiest when we have an outward, rather than an inward focus. It is for the child's ultimate happiness to work at gently leading her toward being aware of the feelings of those with whom she comes in contact.

It is an un-special need to have an outward focus and to know that my life can be a blessing to those around me.

We're All Fragile Jars

There's a sense in which we are all "in the same boat." We are all weak, and to some degree, we all have disabilities and weaknesses. That's because we are made, as the Bible points out, of "houses of clay" (Job 4:19). We are literally eternal beings who are for a time wrapped in weak human flesh. But there is a treasure inside each human, and for those who know God, a double treasure. Everyone has the treasure of being made in the Creator's own likeness, and to those who invite Him to indwell them, they have the unspeakable treasure of housing the living God. Second Corinthians 4:7 says, "We have this treasure in earthen vessels, so that the surpassing greatness of the power will be of God and not from ourselves." A couple Greek words from this verse help us to get the picture: *skeuous* basically means "jar" and *ostrakinos* is defined as "earthenware with the added suggestion of frailty."

What does this have to do with kids who have special needs reaching out to others in friendship? If your child has harder-than-average challenges, what an opportunity for you as a parent or caregiver to help this young person understand that he has a treasure inside of him, a treasure that is only made more evident by weakness! He may feel in his heart that because of his limitations, he has nothing to offer, and therefore why reach out to others? He may *think* he has nothing to offer, but he is so wrong!

Let me ask you, have you ever been greeted by a child who has special needs, say maybe one who has Down syndrome or a young person in a wheelchair, with a bright and sincere smile coming from a radiant face? Did not that smile stir your heart and encourage your soul? Likely it did! Kids whose "jars" are more fragile than most can touch hearts with the smallest gestures. It's kind of like we all have cracks in our "jars," and perhaps the bigger the crack, the more light is able to shine through—perhaps the weaker jars demonstrate that there is more going on than what's on the outside. The treasure is on the inside!

Think of the encouragement you can impart to your son or daughter by helping them realize that God can shine in their lives, and even specifically through their disability, in a way that goes beyond the norm, a way that is designed to show that God's light can shine even through a clay jar, and perhaps especially through a "jar," or body, that is more vulnerable than most. Why? Because it's not the outside that matters most, it's what is inside of the soul!

Someday, we as believers will have bodies that reflect all the fullness of the glory of God, when He raises us "imperishable" and "in glory" as described in 1 Corinthians chapter 15. For now, the glory that God displays in His people has to sort of shine through the cracks of the earthen vessel! This is why the apostle Paul said, "When I am weak, then I am strong" (2 Corinthians 12:10). John Piper, when commenting in a sermon on 2 Corinthians 12, defined this "weakness" discussed in the passage. He said, "Weaknesses are not sins but experiences and situations, circumstances, and wounds that are hard to bear and that we can't remove." I can't think of a better description of the weaknesses that individuals who have special needs are called to carry.

Tell your child about the treasure that is inside of him. Talk to him about it, even if he seems not to understand or be listening. How often as a parent I realized years later that my kids were listening and did understand after all! Help this child realize that small things matter: a smile, a listening ear, a question showing concern, or even just bright eyes that communicate "I'm glad to see you."

Everett Hale once said, "I cannot do everything, but I can still do something." Everyone can do something to encourage another person—everyone who has the smallest ability to relate to others can do something. And those whose "vessels" are weakest can perhaps do more than anyone to demonstrate that the life of an individual is in the soul, a soul which remains completely intact, though the body may be fragile.

It is an un-special need to know that I have a part of me, a treasure on the inside, that cannot be destroyed or diminished by physical or cognitive weakness. It is an un-special need to know that I can enrich the lives of others by using the gifts that God has put into my soul!

As the quotes indicate at the beginning of this chapter, finding a friend is largely a matter of being a friend. It doesn't always work "tit for tat," in that there will always be individuals who don't respond to gestures of friendship; but in the big picture, your child will be blessed with respect-based relationships when he or she is equipped with the tools of learning to *be* a friend.

Everyone Hurts

There are certain things that all human beings have in common. One of those things is we all live in a fallen world and to one degree or another have experienced the pain of it.

It was interesting to me to observe the people who were attracted to Brad—neighbors, acquaintances, people in a grocery line. With each person who showed interest in my son, I had a distinct feeling that although they cared about him, they also had a need met in their own hearts in relating to him. It was like they were silently saying, "You know what it is like to hurt, and I am hurting too." I think that is why so often it was adults who showed an interest, because they had lived long enough to experience some significant pain and disappointment. Our culture is full of individuals who have learned the art of looking "together," of hiding their sorrow, of saying a cheerful "great!" when asked how they are doing. But a person with a disability is not able to hide behind a facade of "everything is just fine with me." And many people are attracted to someone who understands what it means to hurt.

This can actually be a platform for friendship in a young person who has obvious limitations. If you walk in the midst of a group of teens, for example, they all try their hardest to look so cool. Yet, some of them have parents going through divorce, some are neglected or abused, some have hidden disabilities that they live with and that cause them great pain. If a young person who has an obvious disability can learn to ask, "How are things going with you?" and then really listen and offer a sympathetic look or word of kindness, this can be a friendship builder among his peers. Admittedly, many young people will not be willing to open up on the first try. But there will be those who are willing to share their burdens, and will be glad to have a listening ear to do so.

If your child is verbal, older, and has some degree of maturity, she can learn to lend a sympathetic ear to her peers. But even young kids or kids who have serious limitations can be taught that other people have hurts and challenges in their lives, even though these difficulties may not show as much as theirs might. This will build a foundation for becoming a compassionate person and avoiding the misconception that just because other people's hurts, loneliness, and pain don't show, that they don't have any.

It's not a bad exercise for even us as adults, when we meet someone, to say to ourselves, "Like me, this person has known (to one degree or another) sadness, loneliness, and pain." It makes for a compassionate start to a relationship; and if we can teach our kids to do that, at whatever level they can understand, it will help them become a compassionate person as well. And nothing lends itself to friendship that is built on respect like *mutual* compassion.

Time to Soar

Pray about changing your mindset.

Perhaps you have been focusing on the dilemma of your child having friends, which is difficult for him or her to do. Rather, ask God to help you put your focus and efforts on helping your child *be* a friend. Don't expect immediate results, but as it says in Ecclesiastes 11:1, "Cast your bread upon the waters, for you will find it after many days" (ESV). Set your mind and heart toward helping your child to learn to "cast bread on the waters," that is, to make others feel valued, and watch that love return to them over time.

*Role-play with your kids!

Give them ideas, perhaps a list, of questions and comments that make two-way conversations more likely. Role-play, being the other person. Let your son or daughter practice with you, asking questions such as, "What's new with you?" And remind them to make an effort to really listen to the answer.

*Try it yourself.

Next time you meet someone new, or perhaps speak with someone who seems very "together," try saying to yourself before you speak, "Like me, this person has known (or will in the future know) sadness, loneliness, and pain." See if you are not more able to give an encouraging word and an understanding gaze to this person because of it.

KIDZ

Is it hard for you to find friends? I have bad news and good news (mostly good news) for you! The bad news is that finding friends is not something you can control. You can't just say, "I'm going to go find a bunch of people today who will be my friends."

But here's the good news! You can't make people be your friend, but you can always, always choose to **be** a friend. And most often when you decide to be a friend to other people, without demanding anything in return, you will find that they start to be friendly toward you!

Do you want to know the best way to make someone feel important? It's by listening to him or her. Talking is good, but only after you have been a good listener. My older son Ricky as a little boy was a talker! He liked people (and still does) and he felt that talking (and talking and talking) was the way to have relationships with people.

One day, I suggested to him, "How about when dad comes home, before you start talking to him, you say, 'Dad, tell me about your day!'" He did that. And when he grew up, he started asking those kinds of questions without being told. He is now a really great listener and people often come to him just to be listened to!

Being a good listener and caring about what someone says is on the tip-top of the list of how to be a good friend!

FIVE

I Need to Know That My Parents Delight in Me

*The supreme happiness of life
is the conviction that we are loved.*
VICTOR HUGO

Probably the un-special need that is felt the deepest in a child who has special challenges is the need to be loved. I think we all understand that. But do we understand that this child needs not only to be loved, but taking it a step further, to be an object of delight, particularly by his or her parents? In fact, each one of us has a need deep inside to know that someone delights in who we are.

This chapter will be a little different, and I think you'll enjoy the variety. I'm going to allow you the pleasure of meeting two of my favorite people, my dear friend Karen Leonard and my wonderful husband, Mike.

We'll start with Karen: She and I go way back to college days, and we have stayed friends through thick and thin. God gave us many points of commonality in our long-standing friendship, one being that we both were moms to kids who had harder-than-average challenges.

Karen is wife to her husband Jim (who is a pastor), mom to her son Steven; she is a professional counselor in West Los Angeles, and a fabulous speaker, usually to groups of moms.

Following are excerpts from a talk Karen gave, "Delighting in Your Child":

My husband and I have a fascinating marriage— lots of strengths, plenty of weaknesses, and definitely not easy.

After a couple of rocky years in our marriage, my husband came home one night and announced that he had married me so that he could minister to me. My jaw dropped and I was not thrilled. He was shocked that I was not thrilled. After hours of heated discussion, I began to understand that he was trying to tell me that he was committed to me through thick and thin. I did appreciate that. BUT, I didn't want to only be his ministry, or a stalwart commitment or obligation. I wanted to know that he appreciated my wit, my personality, my unique characteristics that no one else had. I wanted to know that he liked being with me, that I was a DELIGHT to him. The kind of love that is a committed choice is important for any lasting relationship, and ours has lasted over twenty-one years. But I wanted more. Our children want more. We all want more.

The dictionary definition of delight is: to affect with great pleasure; to please highly. The bottom line is: This word, this emotion, this action verb is an awesome gift we are given and that we have the opportunity to give to our kids.

In Psalm 18:16-19, David tells of how God

delivered him from some very threatening circumstances and foes:

> *He sent from on high, He took me; he drew me out of many waters. He rescued me from my strong enemy and from those who hated me, for they were too mighty for me. They confronted me in the day of my calamity, but the* LORD *was my support, He brought me out into a broad place;* **He rescued me, because he delighted in me.** (ESV)

Look at the verbs: God the Father sent, drew, rescued, and supported. He did all these actions toward David because He delighted in David. I love that!

There are many things that can dampen our delight toward our kids, that can trip us up in our daily ability to demonstrate the kind of gladness that will make our child's heart blossom, but let's look at a few up close:

Delight Killers

Not spending time with God so that we know He delights in us. It is our number one priority to know Him, yet most people do not have a regular quiet time. Being a mom, especially a "special mom" is a 24/7 calling. It will always be hard to have a regular time with God. But there is a difference between difficult and impossible. It is God's will that we meet Him daily, connect with Him, be in His Word—so difficult, yes—impossible, absolutely not.

You may have to be creative! Susanna Wesley had ten children, and she advised them that when her apron was over her head, she was not to be disturbed because she was having prayer time!

My friend Bev puts an empty teacup on her kitchen counter to remind herself that it's time for tea and her time to be with God. My former roommate Kathy bought a coffeemaker with a timer that would grind beans and then make fresh coffee. The clamor of the grinding beans woke her, the aroma of freshly brewed coffee motivated her to rise early to meet with God. These ideas worked for these ladies. They may not be "your cup of tea (or java)," but you can be just as creative in figuring out what works for you.

Remember what Jesus said, "As the Father has loved me, so have I loved you. Abide in my love" (John 15:9, esv), or "Come to me, all you who are weary and burdened, and I will give you rest" (Matthew 11:28, niv).

We know He wants to be with us, to have intimate relationship with us. So ask Him for creativity and determination. He will answer you. You will begin to deeply understand how much He desires you and delights in you.

Remember, you and I can never delight in our kids fully until we are spending time with the God who delights in us.

He will exult over you with joy,
He will be quiet in His love,

He will rejoice over you with shouts of joy.
(Zephaniah 3:17)

Comparison is another potential delight killer!

I actually feel like a comparison addict sometimes!
Without even trying, I'm comparing myself to others
in every way, shape, and form. And most of the time
in the silliest avenues possible. The other day I was
watching a woman speaker and noticed she had great
arms: tight and muscular. Then I looked at my own
arms, not so tight and muscular. Then, with a fair
amount of angst, I realized that I would be speaking
up in front of a group in a few days (obviously, not
enough time to get in shape). And I thought, "Maybe
others will be looking at my arms instead of listening
to my words." My mature way of dealing with that
comparison—I wore long sleeves!

We can laugh at the silly comparisons. However,
when it comes to our children, it is a whole different
story. Comparisons between typical and atypical
children can be discouraging and even painful when
our kids continually come up short of our society's
standard of measure.

Imagine in our mind apples and oranges. Every
single comparison we make with another person is like
comparing apples and oranges. Every one of us has a
different calling and a unique set of gifts and talents,
not only for this life, but for the next. It is impossible
to compare ourselves with others in any healthy or
intelligent manner when God's standard of measure
and His calling for each of us is multidimensional and
far beyond our understanding.

In John 21:20-22 Jesus was most definitely making a strong statement regarding comparisons. When Peter asked about what was up for John, Jesus said to him, "If it is my will that he remain until I come, what is that to you? You follow me!" (ESV).

Every time you and I are tempted to compare ourselves, our children, our situation with another human being, we need to picture apples and oranges and hear Jesus' words, "YOU follow Me!"

Guilt can strangle the life out of delight! Before I was a mom, I only knew one thing about guilt—how to spell it. After I became the mother of my lovely son, I knew how it felt, smelled, and tasted on what seemed like a daily basis.

For example, when we discovered that Steven struggled with attention and auditory processing issues, I was completely baptized into the abyss of mom-guilt. I went over every single thing I might have done wrong while pregnant. Foremost on the list was my addiction (and I kid you not) to Cheez-Its my first trimester. Not only did they taste incredible, but they helped my nauseous stomach.

I could share more! Suffice to say, if you have felt a particular kind of guilt, I probably have too.

Ambiguous guilt is not from God, and He encourages us to take control of our thoughts. Second Corinthians 10:5 says that we are to bring every thought captive to the obedience of Christ. Guilt is never helpful and is always a hindrance to delight.

Much of the time, our parent guilt is ambiguous, but sometimes, we feel guilty because we really are! At those times, we have the freedom in Christ to confess our sins and be forgiven. First John 1:9 says, "If we confess our sins, he is faithful and just to forgive us our sins and to cleanse us from all unrighteousness" (ESV).

How to Grow in Delight

Psalm 139 is clear that nothing about our children is a mistake:

> *For you formed my inward parts; you knitted*
> *me together in my mother's womb. I praise*
> *you, for I am fearfully and wonderfully made.*
> *Wonderful are your works; my soul knows it*
> *very well. My frame was not hidden from you,*
> *when I was being made in secret.*
> (verses 13-15, ESV)

God has made your child—body and soul. You may want someone a little different—more athletic, more academic, less strong-willed, calmer, sweeter, taller, darker, lighter, funnier...perhaps more typical.

I speak from hard-earned experience and difficult choices when I say, it is imperative to develop a mindset toward your child that sees the beauty of his personality and the gifts and talents God has given him. We can't control much in this life, but we sure can choose what we dwell on and think about all day long.

If I were honest with you, I'd tell you how often my husband had to remind me that my thoughts were miles from enjoyment (like about 1,000 miles). And I didn't want to hear it. I would always counter with how natural it is for a mom to worry about her child's future and just about everything else that related to the "baby she bore." I even told him that if he would have the courtesy to worry a little more, I'd be free to worry a little less.

I did know deep down, way down, almost out of my conscious awareness, that he was right, and I did see firsthand the pride and joy he had with our son. But that just bugged me! For crying out loud, our son did have some challenges!

His response: "Everyone has challenges, some more, some less. Our son is a gift, and God means for us to enjoy our gift." I understood his logic, but my emotions didn't respond to logic.

Thankfully, God began to speak to my heart: "You can either spend your life in anxiety, or invest it in joy." Certainly, my focus and emotions didn't change in a split second, but change they did. And the difference was dramatic. When God says to think on whatever is true, pure, lovely, commendable, excellent, or worthy of praise in Philippians chapter 4, He isn't just giving us nice ideas. He is exhorting us to live according to the way we were created and according to that which brings and gives peace and joy.

As I focused on my son's humor, smile, sparkling eyes, imagination, generosity, love of writing and reading, my life changed and so did my relationship with my son.

My encouragement to you is to work hard to change your focus, and then to change your words. Talk about your son or daughter's strengths with others and especially with your child.

Certainly, parents who have children with harder-than-average challenges are often bombarded with everything the child can't do or accomplish, and the seemingly never-ending therapy appointments and well-meaning advice.

Hence, we can forget that our child has strengths, gifts, talents, and a calling, and God expects and desires that every child use these gifts. Your child and my child are not only called to bless the world with their gifts, they desperately desire to give what they have been given. But it's so difficult and sometimes seemingly impossible to use or give something that no one, especially mom and dad, has ever recognized or admired.

Marcus Buckingham wrote a book entitled *Now, Discover Your Strengths.* It's a book that encourages corporations and businesses to bring out the best in their employees. But the principles certainly apply to parenting. He said, "Unfortunately, most of us have little sense of our talents and strengths, much less the ability to build our lives around them. Instead, guided by...psychology's fascination with pathology, we become experts in our weaknesses and spend our lives trying to repair these flaws, while our strengths lie dormant and neglected."[1]

May We Not Lose Precious Years

I have to tell you that I love the movie *Mr. Holland's Opus.* A brief summary of the movie: Mr. Holland was very concerned about his life work counting for something great. His life was music. The good

side of Mr. Holland came out in the movie in that
he spent himself on the students in his music class
and lost the opportunity to do that "great" musical
accomplishment he had dreamed of. The foolish part
of Mr. Holland came out when his son was born
deaf, and he pretty much completely rejected him
because his son's deafness didn't fit with his life goal
of musical achievement.

To make a long story short, when Mr. Holland's
son, Cole, was a teenager, the light finally went on.
As Larry Crabb put it in his book *Connecting*, "The
most touching moment in this movie comes when Mr.
Holland finally recognizes in his teenage son a passion
for life that exists beneath his hearing loss. It finally
dawns on Mr. Holland that Cole longs to be part of his
father's life, and could be, through a medium far richer
than music, a medium that deafness can't block."[2]

Every parent who has a child with "issues," a child
outside the box of "typical," understands the loss of
a dream, the fear of isolation and rejection, and the
heartache of not connecting on levels they have longed
to connect on. But what we do with that initial fear,
shock, and disappointment is crucial.

What we can learn from Mr. Holland's tragic loss
of years with his son is, now is the time to celebrate
the children God has given us. Today is the day to
demonstrate that they have value, not only in our eyes,
but in God's heart.

Likely if our children don't see this delight on our
faces, they will struggle to believe they have value to
God, and every other relationship they encounter.

May we not lose precious years focusing on the

loss of our dreams. May we realize that our child's
disability or issue cannot block God's good purpose
for that young person's life and for our relationship
with him.

Karen has grown in her commitment and ability to fully delight
in her son—not that she didn't always love her son, but those
"delight killers" are probably common to most "special parents."
The limited time, the guilt, the constant temptation to compare
can eat away at the delight in our hearts.

Dads face these struggles in a different way, but they too
must be determined to delight in the child who poses more of a
constant challenge and who can unintentionally be a drain on
time, finances, emotions, and energy. The next part of this chapter will be Mike Linder sharing how he came to be committed
to delighting in his children even more than in his career and
other pursuits—how he came to realize the utter importance of
it, and how he endeavored to overcome the obstacles involved
in demonstrating this delight in day-to-day life:

Missing the Important Stuff

Sometimes life gets busy and we miss the important
stuff—like delighting in our kids.

I have a clear memory of my daughter and me,
just the two of us, going together to return the rental
truck we had used to move to a different state. The
drop-off place was in a town over an hour away, so
we had plenty of time to relate, towing the trailer and
driving across the open fields of the countryside. Being
the sharp conversationalist that I am, I would say in a
sing-songy way, "Kri-stie!" and she would reply in the

same singy-songy tone, "Da-doo!" On the way back, we stopped to eat at Dairy Queen, a top-tier restaurant for a three-year-old, making it an outing to remember.

Later, I would come to realize that this was our first and only outing with just the two of us. All of my daughter Kristie's life, I had been working six days a week and holidays, too busy to get away much with my family, focused more on my career. You might say, I was delighting in my successful career. I had just left that job to make home more of a priority, but it came too late for my first child. A few weeks later, Kristie got very sick, slipped into a coma, and five weeks later, passed away.

That outing was a time to remember because it afforded the opportunity for me to express to my daughter how I delighted in her. The one-on-one time doing something together communicated, "I want you to be with me. I don't want to miss an opportunity to be together."

I have learned, to a large degree the hard way, that our kids have an un-special need for us to delight in them. I can never get that lost opportunity back with my daughter, but God used that sadness in my life to help me to be more intentional with my sons.

Let me share some practical ways of "delighting" that have worked for me...

Let's Do This!

I like Home Depot better than other home improvement stores because it purposely appeals to men. It's a "big box" store with the slogan "Let's

Do This!" which implies the idea of "stop being intimidated and stop procrastinating and do what you really want to do."

When you're a dad to a kid with special needs, the thought of being an active dad can sometimes seem more intimidating than pulling out plumbing or finishing a basement. That slogan, "Let's Do This," pretty aptly describes the big breath a man has to take and the step of determination that goes into trying to do typical things with a kid who has atypical needs. Yet, if a dad is going to show delight in his son or daughter, he has to come up with ideas and have the attitude of "Let's Do This!"

Here's a start of my journal from late March many years ago:

> *"After a week of rain the sun came out for the weekend and the weather warmed up so Rick, Brad, and I went on a hike." And the closing line, "Brad's boots leaked like a sieve and were full of water when we got home, and a good time was had by all!"*

Brad couldn't walk, let alone hike, so how does a kid with that kind of disability get leaky boots full of water from wading in a creek?

Our family had found an all-terrain stroller, which proved to live up to its name! Brad was five years old at the time, and small for his age, so it served us well for going "off road." This tool for traversing bumpy ground along with "dad power" opened up a world of delighting together: building dams in a stream, wandering through the woods, floating stick boats through "rapids," and the joy of getting wet and dirty in the great outdoors.

These kinds of adventures are not likely to come easy for us dads when our kids have special needs, no matter what form they might take. Just to show you how exhausted I was after an adventure like that: There's a line in the above journal entry that says we left the binoculars on a rock in the creek but I was too tired to go back for them. If you knew how frugal I am, you'd know that this old dad was tired!

But before we write something off with "my child's special challenge won't allow it," why not consider acting on the slogan "Let's Do This!"? We will likely surprise ourselves when we do.

It's an un-special need to get out into the great outdoors somehow, someway, and to have someone delight in you enough to make it happen.

Another thing that worked for us was tent and cabin camping. It requires some extra thinking to come up with lots of activities for the tent campsite when mobility is a problem. There were some Crazy-Eight card game marathons where the number of games got into the dozens. When the work of pulling off tent camping gets a little overwhelming, cabins are a great alternative and can lead to memory-making adventures together.

The planning required is significant to make these outdoor adventures happen, and the resolve of "Let's Do This!" has to be committed to time and time again.

But the result is worth it when our children get the message, "I love these special places and I wouldn't miss out on sharing them with you because I delight in you." On top of that we expose our special kids to the message of God's creation as Psalm 19:1-2 says, "The heavens are telling of the glory of God; and their expanse is declaring the work of His hands. Day to day pours forth speech, and night to night reveals knowledge."

Delighting in Hard Times

"My hero was my dad who helped me a lot from time to time." This is the first line of an English assignment my son had in junior high school, and which I now treasure and have framed on my office wall. The short essay talks about dad being there to help during the many surgeries at Children's Hospital in San Diego.

Can we delight in being with our child in the hardships they face? One of the gifts we can give is to communicate, "I'm glad to be here with you and to share the load of this difficult time. This is not a chore for me; it is not a burden; I wouldn't be anywhere else but here with you."

Coming to that point is definitely a decision and a determined focus. For example, the strain of traveling to San Diego for the dozen or so surgeries held sacrifices for all of us in the family. We were required to take what would have been family vacation time nearly every year; we had the expense of hotels, food, and of course, the medical bills; Beverly took the day shift, so she was in a hospital room during the sunshine part of the day; Ricky came to the hospital intermittently, and then had to find ways to entertain himself; and I took the night and early morning shift. I'm convinced that part of the nurses' training is to make sure that no one sleeps more than an hour at a time at night! And of course, Brad had the very worst of the whole thing, being in pain and laid up for days or weeks at a time.

Still, we all tried to communicate to Bradley, "I am not glad for this difficulty, but I am glad to be walking through it with you."

What kinds of things can communicate this delight even during hard times? For me as a dad, specifically during the hospital times, it was surfing channels until we found something good to watch, and then getting excited over it and bringing a spirit of joy to the room, rather than gloom. Or it meant reading a book with gusto or finding a way to play cards, even when back surgery made positioning awkward.

And then there were times that were so difficult that movies, games, and stories just were not enough to bring any comfort. At those times, the delighting showed itself in holding a hand and whispering words of affirmation.

You may have a completely different situation. Perhaps medical issues aren't the source of your child's hardships. But no matter what form it takes, delighting in kids during tough times will penetrate their hearts with a message of "You're not a burden to me, and I'm glad to be here to support you."

It is an un-special need to be delighted in by parents, even when, maybe especially when, times are hard.

I have a reminder of that on the wall of my office.

Apprentice

So much of life is work! If our kids are not part of what we do when we are working, they are relegated to a much smaller part of our lives. I have a confession to make—it was always hard for me to include my kids in my projects. It's so much easier to get something done by myself! Kids just tend to get in the way. But fortunately, I learned before it was too late that passing on to kids the satisfaction of work well-done is part of delighting in them. And when the kids got older, I was actually relieved of some labor!

As Ricky grew up, I could include him in big jobs, like installing a laminate wood floor, but including Brad was tougher. The temptation was to put him in his room each time there was a project and give him something to entertain himself with. But there are ways to allow most kids to participate. Brad could hold a paintbrush in his platform walker and actually learned to paint a piece of wall pretty well! He could also hold a hose while sitting in his wheelchair and water while I did yard work. He even got pretty good at constructing PBJs when mom was out and about on a Saturday afternoon and dad was home in charge of lunch!

Folding laundry was one job I didn't mind sharing one bit! We have photos of all of us boys hard at work folding clothes and having fellowship in the process.

A seven-year-old who can't stand, walk, or even lift most anything did fine with a card table loaded with washcloths and hand towels. Folding laundry is just a little thing, but to a kid, it yields big satisfaction in knowing that he has helped make the household run smoother and relieved others of some chores. He won't even complain much when it is a group event!

There may be opportunities at the office too. For me, Friday was a good time to bring sub sandwiches to enjoy in the lunchroom with my son. When Bradley was older and more able to focus, he could spend the afternoon doing simple data entry projects that were not of a sensitive nature. It also communicates volumes to a child who has a disability that dad is proud to have him meet his co-workers.

I know that there are different conditions and situations that might make the specific ways I involved the kids in work difficult for others. The idea is to get to know your kid until you figure out some ways to be involved in his or her life. And then, do the best you can to communicate delight through giving them the opportunity to find satisfaction in accomplishing something that helps out the family or even others who are not in the family.

Never Too Late to Start Over

Stress and weariness can get to you as a parent, especially when there is a child who has ongoing difficult challenges.

As my son Brad grew into a young man, I found that it became more difficult for me to connect with him. Seasons change. As he struggled in new ways with his disabilities, I was frustrated and had a pattern of coming across to him as being annoyed.

All parents go through these times. Beverly had her time of struggle when Brad was first born. She just couldn't believe that we were given yet another child with a life-threatening disability. It was hard for her to delight in him for the first few months. She felt confused and depressed.

Now it was my turn to struggle. I was committed to my son, but I wasn't delighting in him, and he knew it.

Thank God that His mercies are new every morning and His grace was available to me as I sought Him to change this bad pattern that had developed.

Brad was more than anxious to restore a friendship with his dad, and there wasn't a bit of hesitation when I suggested a new and fun way to reconnect.

We found connection in a fitness game. With the use of a very cumbersome platform walker, Brad was able to get around in large public buildings, such as the community college he was attending. To encourage walking and exercise, we got him a fitness game that worked with a pedometer and a Nintendo game. The breakthrough for our relationship was that it came with *two* pedometers. From the day he got it, till the day he left this earth, we each carried one in our pocket. Every night we would load our results into the Nintendo. It would evaluate how we did that day on our personal walking goals and give us targets for the next day.

What an amazing point of connection that little game gave each day! The high-fives if we hit our goals, the groans if one of us missed our goal by just a fraction, and laughing at the way the game gave encouragement and goals for the next day. And from there, we could relate in other contexts of life because we had re-established our friendship. I still keep my pedometer in my desk drawer.

It is an un-special need to have a relationship not only with mom, but with dad, who may be less inclined to be relational naturally.

Delighting, like most everything in life, is a choice. And for a man, especially, those kinds of choices are easier when there is something concrete, tangible, and physical to help make it happen. Most of us men just aren't apt to sit around and feel sentimental, but when there is something physical to do, it makes the choice of delighting in a child more doable.

The apostle Paul said in Philippians 4:1 that those who were his "charge" were his "joy and crown." I am so grateful that although there were times of struggle and weakness for me as a dad, God gave me grace to place my children where they belonged, as my joy and my crown.

Time to Soar

Watch out for comparing and envy.

Karen mentioned comparing as a "delight killer." Be on alert this week for comparing yourself, your life, and your children to others. Comparing leads to envy. Rick Warren has pointed out that you can't be envious and happy at the same time!

Here's a suggested prayer to help you get started on your resolve not to be envious as a result of comparing:

Dear Lord,
Forgive me for not believing that You have given me
just the life and the children that will be best for me
and ultimately make me happy. I yield to Your infinite
wisdom toward me. Help me to refuse to turn my eyes
in comparison with others, and to refuse to give my
mind to envy. In Jesus' Name. Amen.

Spend some time reflecting on how God delights in you!

Get that cup of coffee or tea and open your Bible, perhaps start with something simple, such as Psalm 23, and meditate on how God delights in His people and His individual children. Then think about practical ways you can demonstrate to your children, especially your special child, that you delight in them.

Just for dads.

Think of something you would like to do with your child who has special needs but have been hesitant to try. Maybe start with the easiest one that you think of, and say to yourself, "Let's Do This!" And then do it!

KIDZ

The Bible says that a wise child brings delight (joy) to his or her parents (see Proverbs 10:1)!

Your parents already love you. You don't need to do anything to earn their love. But there is a way to bring even more joy to their hearts—by being in the habit of making wise choices.

What is wisdom? Well, think of a stack of books, a stack so high that it reaches to the ceiling! Just think if you had all the knowledge in those books right in your head. You'd be really smart, wouldn't you? But even if you were that smart, you wouldn't necessarily be wise!

Wisdom is knowing right from wrong and choosing to do what is right. Sometimes that is a very hard thing to do. Both children and adults fail to be wise many times. But if we ask God to help us, we can grow in making wise choices. And God says in the book of Proverbs that as you improve, you will bring joy and delight to the hearts of your parents. And guess what, you will also bring joy to the heart of God.

Pray that you can grow in your ability to make wise choices. We all need to pray that!

Here's a prayer you could pray:

Dear God,

I want to please You and I want to please my parents. Please help me to make wise choices. Thank You for hearing my prayer. In Jesus' Name. Amen.

SIX

I Need Loving Correction

Do not provoke your children to anger, but bring them up
in the discipline and instruction of the Lord.

EPHESIANS 6:4

Oscar Wilde said, "The best way to make children good is to make them happy." I would like to scramble up that statement a bit and say, "The best way to make children happy is to help them to be good."

Let me explain: First, the definition of "good." Does it mean external behavior? Yes, it means that—but it also means much more. It means understanding right from wrong and developing, over time, a desire to choose what is right. Ultimately, with maturity, it means loving God's ways from the heart. John said, "For this is the love of God, that we keep His commandments; and His commandments are not burdensome" (1 John 5:3). A lofty goal indeed, even for adults! And we learn patience and kindness toward our children by observing the patience and kindness that God has for us as we struggle with the same lesson!

This is how "good" could be defined: to come to love the things that God loves from the heart, and to have behavior that reflects that love. When we, ourselves as well as our children, grow more and more in that direction, we also grow in possessing a God-given joy.

What Is "Loving Correction"?

"Loving correction" is a phrase that may seem contradictory to some, but it is not a contradiction. We tend to think of making sure we "love" our children much more in proportion than we correct or discipline them. But correction is an integral part of love, for it looks not at the short-term only, nor at ensuring that our kids will at every moment feel positively about us, but it looks to the long-term—the child's life when he may not have us around anymore, when he needs conviction and stability in his own soul to traverse the challenges and the joys of this world.

Hebrews 12 says of God, "Whom the Lord loves He disciplines," and it's the same with us as parents, God being our role model as a perfect Father. Have you noticed that God sometimes allows us to question Him or even to be angry at Him? That's because although He cares very much that we love Him, He cares most immediately that we are not allowed to go on a wrong path in life, or to make foolish life decisions. And He knows that eventually, when we realize that He has dealt with us in kindness and wisdom for the long-term, we will love Him more, not less, because of it. And our kids will, in the long-term, love us more, not less, when we consistently bring them to the right paths of life.

This chapter contains a lot of general parenting principles that apply to both the typical child and the child who has special needs. There's a reason for that, as the goals in parenting the special child are the same, although the road getting there may at times be uniquely different.

It is an un-special need to be directed onto the right paths of life by way of loving correction from my parents.

It Takes Time...and Blood, Sweat, and Tears!

How long does it take to create a masterpiece? And how much work and toil goes into it? Michelangelo took four years to paint the ceiling of the Sistine Chapel, which doesn't sound that long until you realize how many hours of his life actually went into it. And looking at the masterful painting on the chapel dome, one might imagine that Michelangelo was in bliss as he worked. But not so, he was nearly tortured by his artful labor; it was tedious and grueling. Here are parts of a poem he wrote to his friend Giovanni during the time that he painted the ceiling:

I've grown a goiter from this trap I'm in,
as cats do from foul water in Lombardy,
My stomach's almost up against my chin,

My beard points skyward,
at my nape the store of memory dangles,
my dripping brush, for jest,
transforms my face into a mosaic floor,

In front I feel my skin stretched lengthwise,
but in back, it crimps and folds.
This is my state:
arched and indented like a Syrian bow

Not to be trusted, though,
are the strange thoughts that through my mind now run,
for who can shoot straight through a crooked gun?

My painting's dead. I'm done.
Giovanni, friend, remove my honor's taint,
I'm not in a good place, I cannot paint.[1]

We can learn a lot from Michelangelo's despairing poem to his friend! For we too, as parents, are called to be God's tool in creating a masterpiece. When our body aches, and our mind seems scattered, and we feel that we can't parent this child, as Michelangelo felt in the last line that he couldn't paint, we need to realize that having a part in a masterpiece calls for tedious days, aching muscles, and mind-grueling work!

God creates the masterpieces who are our children, but He gives us the unbelievable stewardship of making this work of art all that it can be. It is long, laborious work, and the full results are often difficult to see in the short-term.

Although the paintings of Michelangelo were not completed for years, yet all along the way, he saw the progress of his toil, and that drove him to carry on. I'm sure that although the process was exhausting to him, probably some days more than others, the work he produced from his labors was also his greatest joy for he was creating his *magnum opus*, his crowning achievement as an artist.

Likewise, in parenting, as we have the privilege of partnering with God Himself in the completion of a masterpiece, we should see progress all along the way, and that process can also be our greatest joy in life, knowing that we have been an instrument in God's hand in sculpting a human soul.

Part of that "sculpting" is to encourage our child—by personal example and loving correction—to love God and to obey what He has commanded in His Word. As stated above, we learn patience in this task from the patience we ourselves are shown by God as we try and fail and try again, finally achieving some degree of a consistent heart that loves God's ways.

Oh Yes, It Takes Time!

"Aren't you the ones who teach a parenting class here at church?" Ricky's Sunday school teacher felt the need to kind of "rub it in" when we arrived to pick up our son after preschool class. How do you respond to a question like that when your child is in process but the fruit of your labors are not yet evident to the onlooker?

Ricky, was a delight to us, but let me tell you, he was hyperactive as a child (and still is to some degree; he takes after his mom in that way!). Whether it was Sunday school or story time at the library, Ricky was the dash of light that you would see running around rather than sitting nicely in the "criss-cross applesauce, spoon in the bowl" position!

But we were working on things at home. Ricky had "towel time" where he sat cross-legged on a towel and listened to his favorite music. We started at five minutes and worked up to twenty minutes, and eventually, Ricky learned to sit! Yes, he had to *learn* to sit; it didn't come naturally like it did to some of the other kids. And eventually, we saw the fruit of our labor, but it did take time!

Although in some cases parents are not providing the boundaries at home that their special child needs, it is equally true that some are, and that the results of that discipline and instruction take time. The human heart is not something that usually changes instantly, nor do the physical impulses of many kids come easily under control. Chuck Swindoll has said, "I've never met anyone who became instantly mature. It's a pain staking process that God takes us through. And it includes such things as waiting, failing, losing, and being misunderstood— each calling for extra doses of perseverance."[2] That applies to us as adults, and it certainly applies to our kids. So if you're doing the right thing, keep up the good work! It will pay off as you seek God's wisdom daily. And by the way, don't forget to offer to help that Sunday school teacher or classroom teacher who may be struggling with your child while he or she is "in process"!

Just to give you a little "fast forward," Ricky is now twenty-five years old, happily married, and has good employment where he has done a great job of channeling his hyper-energy toward helping people at a fast pace. In fact, he works at a "help desk" where employees call all day with computer questions. When I visited his work, his boss told me that when Ricky is at the help desk, he can rest assured that people are being genuinely cared for.

He was a masterpiece in the making all along...*all kids are!*

The happy truth is that we are not trying to change our kids' basic makeup as a person, but only to help them channel and refine their personality traits, developing strong character, in order to become all that God created them to be.

I used to think that raising kids was like baking a cake. You put in this and that ingredient, you put the oven on just the right temperature, you leave it in for the prescribed time, and out comes a perfect cake! But contributing to the making of a masterpiece is not like baking a cake. It is wearisome work at times; it is unpredictable in short-term results; and the end result, although beautifully sculpted by God, may be quite different from what we had pictured in our minds. *In other words, we are not in control.* We as parents are tools in God's hands, and we need to yield to whatever He designs in our kids. We submit to His timing, yet we don't use that as an excuse for a lack of diligence on our part. But we do realize that every child, whether typical or having special issues, is indeed a masterpiece in the making.

I have to chuckle when I read the journal of Ruth Bell Graham (Billy Graham's wife) dated February 14, 1957. It reads,

*Four full-blooded little Grahams. They fight, they yell,
they answer back. When I got up at 6:15 so did Anne
and Franklin, and they fought during the time I have
with the Lord alone. Grumbling, interrupting, slur-
ring one another, impudent to me. So now they're off to
school. I'm in bed with my Bible thinking it through.*

In the article "In Memory of Ruth Bell Graham," Wendy Murray Zoba made these observations about this journal entry:

*Whatever her thoughts were that day, she got through
it, and the Lord evidently hearkened to her prayers. The
"little Grahams" some 40 years thence are "off" again,
this time with more sanctified dispositions. Franklin...
has stepped into his father's shoes at crusades and over-
sees the Billy Graham Evangelistic Association. Ned
inherited his mother's passion for China and manages a
ministry that distributes Bibles there. Anne's preaching
has no less fire and spellbinding force than her father's.
And Bunny and Gigi serve actively in ministry and
writing or speaking. Ruth's prayers during long hours
alone in that house on the mountain with those five kids
(without a husband) seem to have brought in a multi-
plied harvest.*[3]

Yes, it takes time. It takes time for typical kids, and it often takes even more time for kids who have conditions that make progress more difficult. The important thing to remember is that young people do not generally "outgrow" negative behavior and attitudes. Anne Graham Lotz, one of the young Grahams mentioned above, is now a mother and grandmother, and in speaking about how her mother and father raised the kids, particularly in imparting faith, she said, "One underlying fact is that my parents were intentional about it. They did not leave the instruction of biblical truth to the pastor or Sunday school teacher."[4]

"Intentional" means never giving up, never leaving the development of my child solely to the professionals. That is probably why Ruth sat in her bed with her Bible after a tough morning with the kids and pondered what to do! Consistent, loving correction and instruction will be blessed by God. Don't give up!

It is an un-special need to have boundaries in my life, and at the same time to have room and time to grow into the person that God made me to be.

Consequences Are for Making Good Habits

Shakespeare's Hamlet said to the Queen, "Use can almost change the stamp of nature," meaning: External good habits performed consistently can change a person's natural tendencies and inclinations for the better. Or more simply: Good habits can be formed with "use."

It's part of our job to encourage external good habits in a child. It is God who touches the inside of the soul and makes the child *want* to do what is right, with time.

You may be concerned that giving consequences to your kids will result in merely external behavior. And, for a time, that is true. But listen to the wisdom of John Townsend in *Boundaries with Kids*: "The law restrains our out-of-control selves enough so that we can slow down and listen to the message of love."[5] How true that is. A child, an adult, a human being can learn best when our out-of-control impulses have been calmed enough to listen, to reflect, to ponder. It is then that the wonderful teaching of motives, "it's the right thing to do," can finally take hold.

God's wisdom for raising children is demonstrated in the book of Proverbs. For example, Proverbs 13:24 says *"He who withholds his rod (the correction of discipline) hates his son, but he who loves him disciplines him diligently"* (I am using the definition of "his rod" found in the side margin of the NASB). For the intent of this chapter, the issue is not the method of correction, but only that the correction of discipline is lovingly and consistently applied. A very broad definition of "the correction of discipline" might be: *any unpleasant consequence that the child would prefer does not happen again!*

Note in our proverb that discipline, which involves consequences for inappropriate behavior, is not a violation of love, but rather an expression of love from a parent! Why? Because it is not (or at least it shouldn't be) about us. It's about the child's present and future happiness—her ability to get along with others, her gaining self-control so that she can lay hold of her dreams in life, her peace of mind and heart as she learns to walk in God's ways that He has set forth in His Word.

Parents Should Be Strategists Too!

When we think of strategists, we might think of military officers, or perhaps professionals who are seeking to surge ahead in their field. But parents need to be strategists every bit as much as professionals!

My long-distance friend Belinda Letchford, who home-schools her children from her "outback" home in Australia, has thought long and hard about how to customize child training for her son Daniel, who has some issues that make his behavior and learning style atypical.

Here are some things she shared on one of our Special Heart workshop videos concerning custom-designing parenting for the special child:

> *Jesus holds us to the same standard—to love the Lord your God with all your heart, soul, mind, and strength, and to love your neighbor as yourself. This truth has remained pivotal in our parenting. The standard of God's Word remains the same for each child; yet the journey is going to look different.*

> *There have been many times when I have simply not known what to do next. I have prayed that God would give me parenting strategies outside the box, outside my personality preferences, outside my experiences—that He would show me how to teach Daniel as an individual.*

> *I don't ever want to diminish how hard it is for Daniel, but at the same time, I want him to have the ability to remain flexible and keep his attitude right.*

Belinda describes how preparing her son before a social situation and then staying close to him helps him not to give in to his impulse to have a meltdown from the stress of too much social stimulation:

> *As I stay close to Daniel, I'm able to catch him before he has a meltdown. I give him security while he is processing something that is hard for him. He hears my words and they guide his responses. It is a lifeline that he can grab onto. It is a strategy that he can now own, to handle these social situations on his own.*[6]

"Strategies" for each child will vary, but it is in studying the inclinations of our children and in being intentional about helping to correct them that progress can be made.

It's often much more difficult to consistently correct and teach the heart of special kids; the work involved for parents is literally blood, sweat, and tears! But that hard work is balanced by the joy of knowing that you have helped your beloved child engage in a healthy way with others, for it is this that will free him to touch lives and to express his unique way of glorifying the Creator.

It is an un-special need to receive consequences for behavior and attitudes that would hinder my growth as a person. It is an un-special need to get assistance with strategies that can help me form better habits.

But My Child Already Has a Hard Life

It may be a conscious or even a back-of-the-mind unconscious thought, but often parents are hesitant to correct and discipline a young person who already has a harder-than-average life.

It's not easy to discipline a kid who already has a difficult life! I think of our daughter, Kristie. Although at birth, the doctor told us that because of her severe muscle condition she would never talk, she turned out to be quite a chatterbox by age two. Her chattering was mostly delightful, but she had gotten in the habit of saying "Oh yuk!" when food was served that she preferred not to eat. We told her that she must never say "Oh yuk" when she was given food, and *especially* not if that food was served at someone's home who invited us to dinner. She was instructed that there would be a consequence if she exclaimed in that way, explaining as well the "whys" of not offending the person who prepared the food.

The moment of truth came when we were invited to a bachelor's home for a dinner he had cooked himself. He placed the Shepherd's Pie in the middle of the table and went back to the kitchen to gather the rest of the meal. Little Kristie looked at the dreaded dish, and at her parents whom she knew meant business, and after taking a deep breath reminded herself in a sing-songy voice, "Don't say 'Oh yu-uk!" Mike and I tried to stifle our laughter with little success.

If Kristie had not obeyed us, how could we have been so cruel to impose a negative consequence on this sweet little girl, and a sweet little girl with a disability yet? It's because we were thinking of her long-term good, of her ability to fit in later in life, of her gaining sensitivity to the feelings of others.

At that time we didn't realize that Kristie would leave this earth by the time she was three years old, but we don't regret the times that we held her to account. It was just another way of expressing our love for her; she knew it, and she couldn't have had a happier home life.

We applied loving discipline to all of our three children, all the while considering their temperaments and bents. Some kids need a little firmer application of correction, some respond with much less firmness or even simply to a verbal admonition. But they all need consistent correction!

Don't think you're making life harder for your son or daughter who has a disability when you hold them to account. Remember, what's really hard is to grow up and not know how to respond to people in a way that makes them want to be around you. Think long-term!

Here's a verse to cling to in gaining wisdom for finding a balance in parenting, especially with kids who have special needs:

*Do not let **kindness** and **truth** leave you;*
Bind them around your neck,
Write them on the tablet of your heart.
Proverbs 3:3

Some Suggested Do's and Don'ts

Some of these do's and don'ts are directly from God's Word, some from wise parents who have gone before, and some from Mike and myself in the category of "what we have learned, mostly the hard way, through mistakes!"

Do be consistent. There's nothing worse than making a standard of behavior and then letting it go when we're in a good mood, and blowing up about it when we're in a bad mood! The whole issue then becomes mom or dad and their moods!

We can be tempted to become inconsistent when we don't see results. Why bother? It's too much work to be consistent.

Here's a promise for the parent who feels the temptation to waver:

Therefore, my beloved brothers, be steadfast,
immovable, always abounding in the work of the Lord,
knowing that in the Lord your labor is not in vain.
1 Corinthians 15:58, ESV

Do limit the behaviors you work on at any one time. The ultimate goal isn't merely good behavior, rather it is heart-motivated character. None of us is motivated toward improving when we're overwhelmed or if we feel that someone is picking on us about our every move. If you've ever had a boss who picked on you and criticized you with "micromanagement," you know how demotivating that kind of harassment is!

Rather, choose a couple things to work on and give lots of praise when there is improvement. When it's time to correct, do so during times of nonconflict, when the heat isn't on!

It's especially important to limit correction with kids who have autism or any condition that makes overstimulation stressful. Autistic children are very fond of rules. Use that to your advantage, but add the rules slowly, just a couple at a time.

Ephesians 6:4 says this (from *The Living Bible*): "And now a word to you parents. Don't keep on scolding and nagging your children, making them angry and resentful. Rather, bring them up with the loving discipline the Lord himself approves."

Limiting the scope of training to be doable for children will help to keep them from getting angry and frustrated. God gave us some good advice in Ephesians 6:4, to go slowly in establishing rules, nudge forward gently but firmly, and do a lot of nurturing along the way.

Do focus on the offense and not on the person. Harold Hulbert said, "Children need love, especially when they don't deserve it." This means never insult your child. Don't say things like, "What's wrong with you anyway?" Try not to connect the bad behavior to your daughter or son's person. Don't attack who they are; correct what they do.

Someone has said, "As your kids grow up, they may forget what you said, but they will never forget how you made them feel." It is possible to correct behavior without making a young person feel insulted about who they are.

I know that there were times when I made my kids feel bad. Thankfully, it didn't happen often and we are going to slip as parents since we are not perfect people. Still, we should seek to avoid hurting our kids' feelings with all our heart.

Do own up to your own weakness. In *Changes That Heal,* Henry Cloud pointed out, "The sad thing is that many of us come to Christ because we are sinners, and then spend the rest of our lives trying to prove that we are not!"[7]

Don't try to prove you are not a sinner with your kids! Approach your correction with a spirit of "We're all in the same boat." Maybe once in a while tell a story or two of how you messed up as a kid.

The Bible says, "Confess your sins to one another, and pray for one another so that you may be healed" (James 5:16).

Have you ever confessed your sin to your children? It will make it easier for them to receive correction from you if you do.

Do realize that your example is by far more important than anything you say. "Don't worry that children never listen to you. Worry that they are always watching you." There's truth to that advice from Robert Fulghum.

Here are some things we try to teach our kids:

"Be nice to people; share; don't lose your temper; be aware of the feelings of others; do your chores with a happy attitude; don't mope around because you don't get your way; be respectful to those in authority over you; don't interrupt; say please and thank you; don't scream when you're frustrated; don't cuss; do something with your free time besides media; be respectful of other people's property."

These all have adult versions! And our kids look to see if we are living out the adult version of the commands we give them! How much more powerful is a good example than repeated admonishment.

First Peter 5:3 says, "not domineering over those in your charge, but being examples to the flock" (ESV).

And Just a Few Don'ts...

Don't bribe. "If you sit quietly in the shopping cart, there will be doughnuts on the way home." This is the plea of a tired parent! One mom said, "I can't believe what I'll give my kids in return for a little peace and quiet." If you are a parent, especially an "at-home mom," you understand the temptation. Someone has said that having kids is like installing a bowling alley in your head! And how much will parents give? Well, there is an article by Martha C. White entitled "You Spend Over $1,300 a Year Bribing Your Kids." Her studies indicate that 55 percent of parents give their kids a pretty huge amount of money per year for good behavior.[8]

Jim Fay, author of *Parenting with Love and Logic,* said that in place of respect and responsibility, many of today's kids are cultivating a sense of entitlement which is "a prescription for a lifetime of unhappiness."

That is your motivation right there to not bribe your kids. Young people who have never learned the joy of doing the right thing for its own merit are pretty well destined for a miserable life.

Even in cases where there is a very serious disability, bribing is not good for the child. I have seen parents give a screaming young person a cookie to calm her. But why not give her a cookie when she *stops* screaming? Even when there is a pronounced cognitive and/or physical disability involved, the principle is the same: Think of this young person's future when you may not be around anymore, when others will be caring for her. Help her to find ways to communicate that others will not be uncomfortable with. It's important to think of the child's future, no matter what condition he or she may have.

Don't correct your child when you are angry. Dr. Laura Markham said this,

> *Imagine your husband or wife losing their temper and*
> *screaming at you. Now imagine them three times as big*
> *as you, towering over you. Imagine that you depend*
> *on that person completely for your food, shelter, safety,*
> *protection. Imagine they are your primary source of love*
> *and self-confidence and information about the world,*
> *that you have nowhere else to turn. Now take whatever*
> *feelings you have summoned up and magnify them by*
> *a factor of 1000. That is something like what happens*
> *inside your child when you get angry at him.*[9]

It's particularly easy to feel at the end of our rope as "special parents." We're often late for appointments; we carry health and financial worries; we are needing to do for our kids what typical kids can do for themselves; basically, we're tired! So feelings of frustration may not be far beneath the surface at any given time.

There are many ways for parents to control anger, particularly during times of conflict. One of the most helpful is: *Wait until you calm down before correcting your child.* Oh, the difference to a child between a mom or dad who is correcting with a calm voice and one whose voice is out of control! Don't forget that you have a Friend you can always go to on your knees to ask for control and wisdom.

There's another principle that is even better than getting anger under control: *Correct your kids before you are angry!* I know, you don't feel like disciplining a child when you're not angry, but that is definitely the best time to do it. I rarely had to deal with anger in correcting my kids, because I was committed to giving a consequence for an offense that the kids understood beforehand. I didn't even want to give the consequence most of the time! The kids were still cute to me. I wasn't angry. It was difficult to dole out a consequence. But that is so far better than letting things go until we blow our top! The reason I committed myself to being consistent about consequences before anger sets in is that I know when I do get angry, it's not pretty. I come from a yellin' family of origin, and so I didn't even want to get close to that point of being out of control.

Don't use empty words. Remember the old, yet wise adage: *Say what you mean, and mean what you say.* I remember being in a Target store one Saturday morning. Mom and her three or four kids (it was hard to keep track as they were running here and there!) were shopping for the birthday party that was to be that afternoon. Suddenly, the mom, exasperated from the din her kids were making, stopped and said, "If you don't settle down, there will be no birthday party today." I guess the kids' first clue that these were empty words was that mom was continuing to load the shopping cart with birthday party supplies even as she spoke! There was maybe a four-second pause of silence, presumably while the kids evaluated the threat, and then they went about their revelry just as though nothing had been said—because in reality, nothing *had* been said! They were quite used to empty threats.

Don't make your words meaningless! It will only confuse your kids and make them immune to any words of instruction you may try to give.

Proverbs 16:23 says, "The heart of the wise instructs his mouth and adds persuasiveness to his lips." Here's a possible parenting paraphrase of that proverb: Let your heart be wise before God, and let it instruct your mouth to speak only words that have substance. Then you will be able to persuade your kids to listen when you speak!

It is an un-special need for my parents to be intentional, fair, and consistent in correcting and instructing me.

The True Magnum Opus

We have explored in this chapter how our kids are masterpieces in the making. There are kids who look like masterpieces. They are beautiful, talented, popular, gifted, intelligent, socially graced. Maybe our kids don't measure up to "the good life" standards, and so it doesn't seem that they are such a masterpiece after all.

But the masterpiece that God is looking to perfect is on the inside—someone who is cultivating "the fruit of the Spirit" spoken of in Galatians 5:22-23, "love, joy, peace, patience, kindness, goodness, faithfulness, gentleness, and self-control." No disability or limitation can hinder "the person inside" from developing these qualities. This is the goal of our "loving correction," and I believe God considers the development of these qualities to be His magnum opus!

Time to Soar

*Pray that you will have eyes to see your children, especially your special child, as a masterpiece in the making.

Dear Lord,
You have said that we are all a masterpiece of Yours
(Ephesians 2:10), and that does not exclude my child
who has limitations and special challenges. Thank
You that You have given me the privilege as a parent
to help my children discover and become all that You
made them to be. Give me daily wisdom in being
Your instrument for the purpose of bringing out the
masterpiece that dwells within my children. Thank You
for letting me have a part in this, and please give me
eyes to see the incredible value of my kids, each one of
them! Amen.

*Follow Belinda's example and plan "strategies."

Belinda Letchford shared a little of her strategies that help her son from having a meltdown in public due to his feeling stressed in a social situation.

It's always good to have a plan in mind in anticipating troublesome situations that bring out negative behavior in our children. One strategy is to role-play different scenarios that might occur with your child. This will give him the words to say and the actions he can take when he begins to feel out of control.

Brainstorm and think of the strategies that will help your child with his or her specific areas of behavior weakness.

*Look over the do's and don'ts.

Review the Loving Correction do's and don'ts. Choose one or two that you think you could improve on and work on it this week. Like our kids, it helps us as parents when we focus on just one or two areas of improvement at a time!

KIDZ

Do you know what a masterpiece is? *Merriam-Webster's Dictionary* defines it as "a work done with extraordinary skill."

That means that a masterpiece is a work of art done by an artist who is way, way more skilled than many other artists!

God is the "artist" who has made you. He made every detail about you, inside and outside.

Right now, let's talk about how God made you on the inside...your personality and your character. God doesn't want to change your personality, because your personality is what makes you, you. And He is very pleased that you are you and not exactly like anyone else in this world!

So He doesn't want to change your personality, but He does want your character to GROW! What is character? It is the part of you that knows right from wrong and that can grow in choosing what is right before God.

Every artist who creates a masterpiece has a tool. What tool does a painter have? A paintbrush. What tool does someone who draws have? A pencil, or even a crayon.

If God is an artist who is making you, especially your character, into a masterpiece, what tool do you think He uses?

He uses many tools, but mostly, He uses your parents!

My parents??? My parents aren't tools. They are people! Yes, they are people, but your mom and your dad are also tools in God's hand because He uses them to make you and your brothers and sisters to be all that He created you to be.

That is why they teach you right from wrong; they encourage you to make good choices; they correct you when you make wrong choices.

Don't be frustrated when your parents help you grow in character. After all, God is making you into a masterpiece!

SEVEN

I Need to Learn to Have a Peaceful Heart

Peace I leave with you; My peace I give to you;
not as the world gives do I give to you.
Do not let your heart be troubled, nor let it be fearful.

JESUS, John 14:27

Isn't it so that the moment a child is diagnosed with a special condition, at that moment his parents also come to have special needs that other parents don't have? Suddenly, stress levels go beyond "typical" to off the charts. And the un-special needs, such as the nurturing of mind and soul, can get swallowed up in the drama of the new challenge. This chapter will be a little different in that it will begin by addressing one of *your* un-special needs as a parent...the need to have a peaceful heart.

In addressing your need to have a peaceful heart, automatically it will be touching the lives of your children, and specifically of your special child. If your heart is peaceful, in time, your child's heart will likely learn to be peaceful as well.

This is not to lay guilt on you, implying that if your child's heart is agitated, it is your fault. No, some kids have conditions that lend themselves to agitation of mind and heart. Some children seem to literally be born with a disquieted disposition and unsettled reactions to normal life challenges.

But that is not to say that these same kids cannot, over time, learn by way of their parents' example and of gentle instruction how to calm their emotions and responses.

Oxygen Mask

If you've ever flown on a major aircraft, you've heard these words:

> *If you are traveling with a child or someone who*
> *requires assistance, secure your own mask first, and*
> *then assist the other person.*

This is why we as parents can never help our kids to develop habits of peaceful thoughts and controlled responses if we don't first apply our own "oxygen mask," in mastering these qualities ourselves.

So for now, let's focus on the adult version of learning to have a peaceful heart, then explore direct ways to help kids achieve that restful spirit.

Worry, the Strangler

Probably the number one "peace thief" is worry. It's interesting to look at the history of the word *worry*. According to *The American Heritage Dictionary,* the evolution of the word went like this:

The Old English version: The word was *wyrgan* and meant "to strangle."

The Middle English version: The word was *worien* and

had the meaning of "to grasp by the throat with the teeth and lacerate."

The seventeenth-century definition: "to bother, distress, or persecute."

By the nineteenth-century the word was rendered *worry* and, as we know, came to have this meaning: "to cause to feel anxious or distressed."[1]

The earlier definitions of the word help us to see the awful enemy that worry is to our souls! It truly can strangle us, grasp us by the throat, and persecute us!

Jesus, when He walked this earth, gave this advice: "So do not worry about tomorrow; for tomorrow will care for itself. Each day has enough trouble of its own" (Matthew 6:34).

Sounds so simple, yet our problems seem way more complicated than that. But the Son of God, the One of whom the book of Colossians says, "For by Him all things were created, both in the heavens and on earth, visible and invisible, whether thrones or dominions or rulers or authorities—all things have been created through Him and for Him" (1:16), this is the One who tells us not to worry. He knows how complicated our problems and daily challenges are, yet He tells us not to worry about tomorrow, and so much of our worry is about the future.

Having two children in heaven, I think I understand this concept perhaps better than most. I would worry about the future so incessantly concerning my children; now I know that what really mattered is that I enjoy my beloved kids, and that I believe in the sovereignty and goodness of the One who created them and gave them to my husband and me to love.

It isn't only when children leave the earth at a young age that this applies. When your children grow up, you will likely look back and realize that much of what you worried about has worked itself out in one way or another, and if you have trusted

God, you will see that He has directly intervened and shown His goodness in areas that seemed so impossible.

Don't allow this strangling, relentless enemy, Worry, to haunt you and to rob you of precious years to enjoy your children and your life. Ask God to give you grace to trust His simple command, "Do not worry..."

If Only...

It starts at an early age, "If only I didn't have acne, then I would be happy." "If only I were popular, I would be happy." "If only I were married, then I would be content." "If only I *weren't* married, I would be so happy." "If only we lived in a nicer house, then I would feel satisfied." And on and on it goes into old age, unless we are wise enough to stop the "if onlys" and learn to be content, peaceful, and happy *today*.

As parents of kids who have special challenges, many of our "if onlys" revolve around their condition, wishing that things were different, hoping that things might change. There's nothing wrong with seeking improvement in any area, but life is now, and when we waste precious days focusing on our "if onlys," the days add up to years, and we find we have missed out on the life God gave us to enjoy. Jim Elliot, a missionary who served God with his whole heart, no matter what the cost, said this: "Wherever you are, be all there."[2]

I have a clear memory of being a young mom. As I sat on the floor of the bathroom by the toilet cleaning out about the fifth or sixth round of dirty underpants from a child who no longer wanted to wear diapers but had a temporary bowel problem that made him "leaky," I remember thinking, "Lord, when I was in college, I asked You to use my life for Your glory. I told You I would go anywhere or do anything You asked me to do in Your service. But I have to tell You, Lord, this is not what I had in mind!"

Yet, it was what God had for me at that time, and as unglorious as it may have been, God wanted me to realize that serving Him and that significance in life often come in a completely different package than what I might imagine. It's those moments, days, months, and years of being behind the scenes, serving the family God has given us in ways that seem so very lackluster at times, that can be so much more significant for eternity and for God's glory than all of our "if only" dreams put together!

Part of having a peaceful heart is knowing and believing by faith that the world is not passing us by when we are serving our kids, especially the ones who require more attention than usual.

We may watch longingly as other families seem to be living life while we are "stuck" in a life of meeting special needs, but it all comes into perspective when we hear what Jesus had to say about greatness: "Whoever wishes to become great among you shall be your servant, and whoever wishes to be first among you shall be your slave; just as the Son of Man did not come to be served, but to serve" (Matthew 20:26-28).

And even more amazing, in Matthew 25:40, Jesus flashes us to a future scene when He sits as King and when He is rewarding those who have been faithful to serve and meet needs, and says, "The King will answer and say to them, 'Truly I say to you, to the extent that you did it to one of these brothers of Mine, even the least of them, you did it to Me.'"

There is no better use of our time than to serve and care for these young ones whom God has given us; Jesus counts it literally as service to Himself! This should give our hearts great peace when it seems that our life is slipping away from us while others move on to the "good life." Reality exists on a higher plane, one we can't see but that is nevertheless so very real.

Reflection Time and Quiet

Francis Bacon, who was a great thinker, scientist, orator, and author of his time, said, "Silence is the sleep that nourishes wisdom."

Going along with the idea of you as a parent applying your oxygen mask before you can assist your child in having a peaceful heart, there is nothing in this world that contributes to a peaceful heart more than reflection time and quiet.

Ha! Easier said than done, right? I know, but although it may be difficult, it is usually not impossible to find at least little snippets of time to yourself and to be with God.

When I was in the thick of having my kids be completely dependent on me, I would get up at 5:30 a.m. and, while my husband was still home, take a "prayer walk." Oh how much better that is than getting right out of bed and hitting the floor running with mom responsibilities! My brain would have twenty minutes to enjoy fresh air (*very* fresh, especially in the winter!), to cast my cares upon Jesus, and to plan my strategy for the day.

Now that our kids are no longer in the house, I have a little more time freedom, so instead of getting out at 5:30 this morning, I ventured out at 8:00 for a prayer walk in the foothills of the Rockies. Because it rained last night, my feet got really muddy, but then again, it made for a very quiet time as apparently no one else wanted to get their shoes dirty this morning. But muddy shoes was a small price to pay for the view that lay before my eyes, puffy clouds floating over green foothills, Pikes Peak showing majestically from behind, and miles of colorful wildflowers in a dewy meadow before me. As I sat on what I affectionately call my "prayin' rock," I thought of the words to this hymn:

> *When I look down from lofty mountain grandeur,*
> *And hear the brook and feel the gentle breeze,*
> *Then sings my soul, my Savior God, to Thee...!*

The peacefulness of the moment overwhelmed me, but these moments are fleeting. Yet, even now, later in the day, when responsibilities and a much noisier environment threatens my peace, I believe that the time this morning gave stability to my soul and will continue to do so throughout the busy day.

These times of quiet can also be found indoors, in a comfy chair with a hot drink, or even in sneaking away to the bathtub for a warm soak in the evening. Music is a nice touch to bring all the senses into relaxing harmony.

You will have varying degrees of freedom of time, depending on your family's schedule and the level of dependence of your children, but don't miss out on those luscious times of quiet that will rejuvenate your mind and soul for the more difficult stresses of the day. As Francis Bacon said, that quietness will "nourish wisdom."

Receiving While You Sleep

"Think in the morning; act in the noon; eat in the evening; sleep in the night." So instructed poet William Blake.

It's taken me years to get that piece of wisdom down, but I'm getting there.

My tendency is to go to bed and think, when I should be resting. But over the years, I have gained some insight about how to put things in better order, doing my resting at night and my thinking in the morning.

The most helpful practice I have ever found to rest at night is to meditate on some Scripture that I have memorized. If the brain is a vacuum, it will tend to go right to our problems, but filling the mind with wonderful and comforting truth squeezes out the pesky worries and futile efforts to solve problems when the mind is tired and needing some rest.

Here is my favorite psalm to meditate on at night:

Unless the LORD *builds the house,*
They labor in vain who build it;
Unless the LORD *guards the city,*
The watchman keep awake in vain.

It is vain for you to rise up early,
To retire late,
To eat the bread of painful labors;
For He gives to His beloved even in his sleep.
Psalm 127:1-2

This psalm is a reminder that although God wants us to do our part in building and protecting our children, it is "vain" to overdo it, because ultimately He is the One who is accomplishing what needs to be accomplished. The psalm promises that when we trust God enough to just go to sleep, He is working for our benefit and the benefit of those we are concerned about even while we are in restful slumber!

If you are a good sleeper like my husband, who has no trouble falling right to a restful repose the moment his head hits the pillow, it is still beneficial to use those few moments of consciousness to meditate on God's Word. It gives the subconscious something wonderful to mull over during the night.

It is an un-special parent need to put enough focus and attention on herself or himself to gain a settled and restful mind and heart before God.

Now That Your Mask Is On...

Once you have secured your own oxygen mask, so to speak, and have thought through your own strategy for keeping a peaceful heart (and it does take daily strategy!), then you can move on to helping your children to develop such a heart. As it is with us adults, so it is with children—this doesn't happen in a presto moment! But after time of consistently and gently nudging our kids toward having a settled mind and heart, the results of that effort will begin to show.

Begin with Touch

I was in a hospital bed waiting for a "minor surgery" (is there really such a thing?), and being an incurable coward, I noticed that my teeth were chattering and my body was quivering. Yes, I was a little cold in that huge gown they gave me, but mostly, scared. After a few minutes of this, my husband, Mike, reached over and touched my arm. It was like magic! I instantly stopped shaking, my heart rate, which was being monitored, went down significantly, and I learned a life principle I shall never forget— the power of touch!

Our kids who have special needs desperately need a loving touch. Well do I know that this varies from child to child in terms of how to administer that touch. My daughter Kristie loved to be cradled, even as a toddler. My son Brad begged for backrubs at bedtime, which became a pleasant ritual for us, in spite of the rods in his back from surgeries. My son Ricky didn't care for prolonged touch, but would gladly accept a peck on the cheek, a ruffling of his hair, or a playful squeeze of his arm.

Kids with autism and other conditions that create sensory issues have some really tough challenges for parents to deal with when it comes to touch, and I won't try to explore the depths of these. Only to say, that many of the kids who reject touch often will come to welcome certain kinds of touch, especially deep touch (as opposed to light touch) and touch that is announced ahead of time (rather than unexpected touch).

Even when parents have to be patient and persistent about it, I believe that discovering what works in terms of touch for their son or daughter can open a door to helping to bring calm to an agitated heart.

Here is what James Smith, counselor at Willow Tree Christian Counseling in Northern Ireland, says, "Touch is without a doubt one of the most, if not the most powerful means of communication we have available to us as human beings. We may speak, express ourselves through words, tone, and the volume of our voice, or body language, however, nothing comes close to touch."[3]

Jesus so often touched people when He healed them. Once a leper came to Him and asked for healing. Jesus could have sort of zapped him from afar. Who wants to touch someone who has leprosy? But in Matthew 8:3, it says that Jesus reached out and touched the man. Yes, it was the power of the Son of God that healed this individual, but don't you think that this person with such a dreaded contagious disease also had a kind of healing in his soul when another human being was willing to touch him physically? He probably hadn't felt the touch of a human hand in years.

I suspect that the kids who seem least responsive to touch are perhaps the ones who need it most. Don't force it, but keep trying to *discover* the best way to touch, for it can contribute to healing and to calming a disquieted spirit.

"I'm Sorry"

Hannah was new to the high school group, and she was my charge. I was to be her "buddy" during the high school Sunday school class. Having Down syndrome, she had a difficult time keeping up with the bullet-speed conversation of the other high school kids at our round table. Yet, when I would look at her face and ask her questions, she would whisper her simple but well-thought-through answer into my ear.

During one activity, all the kids were instructed to draw something that had to do with the lesson. So Hannah and I each got our big sheet of paper and our colored pencils and drew along with the others. At one point, Hannah got frustrated because her picture wasn't what she hoped it would be, and took a dark pencil and scribbled all over the picture I had drawn. No loss, that's for sure! But because I was wanting her to know how her actions made people feel, I said, "Hannah, that made me feel bad when you scribbled on my picture." She gave me an inquisitive look.

When class ended, her older brother came to pick her up as he always did, and after our good-byes, Hannah kept looking back at me as she neared the door with her brother. Suddenly, she darted back, put her hand over my ear, and whispered, "I'm sorry for scribbling on your picture." I had long forgotten about the incident, but I gave her a hug and accepted her apology. She bounded back to her brother with a joyful skip, looked back at me, and waved with a huge smile on her face, and I returned a big smile to her.

Hannah left with a peaceful heart. Apparently, her parents

wisely instructed Hannah to say "I'm sorry" when she felt unrest in her heart about something she had done. This is not primarily for the benefit of the other person, but mostly for the benefit of the child herself. God has wired us this way.

First John 1:9 tells us to "confess our sins" and that God is then faithful to forgive our sins. Such a small thing, to scribble on a paper...yes, but not a small thing for Hannah to learn how to have the peace of making a relationship right.

Probably the best way to teach a child to say "I'm sorry" is for her to hear those words from her parents when they have made a mistake or done something wrong. These two small words can grow into a humility that will bring the child to pursue a right relationship with both God and people, and nothing makes for a peaceful heart more than that.

The Natural Cure for ADHD

"Who can resist the appeal of a natural ADHD remedy? You don't need to. Go ahead: Open your door, take a breath of fresh air—and treat yourself right with Mother Nature herself."[4] So begins an article by the editors of ADDitude, a support organization for parents of kids with ADHD and learning disabilities.

It's not just ADHD kids who need this natural remedy to anxiety, but autistic children, young people who have cognitive and physical disabilities, kids who have Down syndrome, and typical children as well!

It's wonderful when we are able to calm our kids with touch, perhaps with some lighthearted fun, or sitting on a cozy couch reading, but reality is, we're not always going to be around to provide these comfort-givers. But nature can always be available to a young person, and if they learn to bask in its quiet and enjoy its wonders, a peaceful heart is something that your child can find on his own, even when you are not around. A good dose of vigorous exercise just adds to the calming effect.

The natural world played such a huge part in calming Helen Keller's disquieted spirit. She was agitated most of the time, not knowing what to do with her untamed energy and with the curiosities of her mind. But when her teacher Anne Sullivan exposed her to the surprises and fascinations of nature, her spirit felt that it had found a "happy peer."

> *Long before I learned to do a sum in arithmetic or describe the shape of the earth, Miss Sullivan had taught me to find beauty in fragrant woods, in every blade of grass, and in the curves and dimples of my baby sister's hand. She linked my earliest thoughts with nature, and made me feel that 'birds and flowers and I were happy peers.'*[5]

As she matured, her teacher didn't need to be there anymore for her to find solace and satisfaction in what God had created. She got so acquainted with her "peers" in nature that she could smell colors! If she were among mostly plants, she would know the area was green. She knew the delicate smell of a specifically pink flower. "Catching an unmistakable plant odor, I know everything is green. Pink seems like dainty music notes smooth as apple blossoms drifting down from the boughs."[6]

Nature is probably the most intentional gift that God gave mankind to calm and delight their hearts. You would think King David would be mostly spending time in a royal palace, sitting upon his royal throne. But when you read the Psalms, you see how often he was outdoors, making observations that helped him to handle the pressures he had in his life. Many ascribe Psalm 104 to David, which says, "O LORD, how many are Your works! In wisdom You have made them all" (verse 24).

God gave us all His bountiful creation to enjoy and to soothe our world-weary minds and souls. In modern times, we don't take advantage of this gift as others did in times past. Children would run and play and work out their "wiggles," thus there were fewer problems with hyperactivity and attention deficit. That gift is still available to us. Take advantage of it!

Osmosis

Take it from me, it won't be that long before your kids are adults. So think of the elements discussed in the first part of this chapter, such as letting go of worry, saying no to "if onlys," making quiet and reflection time in your day, and learning to hand over your cares when it's time to sleep, and know that as you perfect these habits in your life consistently, it's likely that your children will pick them up as by osmosis, unconsciously learning how to gain a peaceful heart by watching you. That doesn't mean you have to be perfect. It only means that you can provide a model for your kids when they begin to grow up and need a picture in their minds of what it looks like to choose a restful spirit and a peaceful heart. Please don't see this as a burden, but as a happy opportunity to give your adult children a gift for life!

Wisdom Speaks to a Quiet Heart

In the book of Proverbs, Wisdom is personified, speaking as a person and urging people to come to her and listen:

> *Blessed is the one who listens to me,*
> *watching daily at my gates,*
> *waiting beside my doors.*

*For whoever finds me finds life
      and obtains favor from the LORD.*
(Proverbs 8:34-35, ESV)

Wisdom can only be heard in a quiet heart. For both children and adults, it is quietness that will bring this friend, Wisdom, close enough to hear and to thus "obtain favor from the LORD."

It is an un-special need to learn to relax, unwind, and be settled in body and spirit so that I can hear the "voice" of God and of wisdom speaking to my heart.

Time to Soar

Reject worry!

View any "worry thoughts" as a vicious enemy that wants to strangle the life out of you! Push these thoughts out of your mind with memorized Scripture, by singing an uplifting song, by reading the Bible or some other book that will speak truth and health into your mind.

Discover your favorite way to have reflection time.

Whether it's outdoor time, reading in a cozy chair, even soaking in a warm tub, or any or all of the above, why not start today making a time of quiet that will contribute to you having a peaceful heart.

God's Word is what will fill your mind with peace and let your heart know how much you are loved. I find that when I go into a quiet time saying to myself, "What shall I read today?" I just flounder. But if I am reading a specific book of the Bible, I can say, "Today is Romans chapter 3," and it gives me direction.

Teach your kids to say "I'm sorry."

Don't feel like you're making your kids grovel by encouraging them to say, "I'm sorry," when they offend you or someone else. It's for their benefit mostly that they learn this—for their peace of mind and it also makes for good relationships with others. If they see the example in you, it won't be a humiliating thing to them to utter these words, but it will begin to come naturally and they will feel good about getting things right.

Expressing being sorry can be overdone too. So, if there get to be too many "I'm sorrys," that is part of your teaching. Not every mistake needs to be a big deal. It's a thing of balance. Sometimes, just "Oops, I made a mistake" is sufficient.

Begin or follow through on the habit of getting your kids outside in nature!

In our culture, it's easy to stay inside all day, every day. But that sterile environment and the lack of physical activity that comes with it do not bring health to a child, neither his body, his mind, or his spirit. Even if the adventure is no farther than your backyard, make that yard as appealing and interesting as possible. Many parents have noticed that their kids with ADD do not need their medication when they go for hikes and have freedom to run in open, green spaces. Try to make it a habit to take advantage of the calming and wonderful resource God has given us in His creation.

KIDZ

Do you ever feel stressed? Kind of like troubled, scared, restless, upset, goose-bumpy type of nervous...like you might explode at any minute?

Everyone feels stressed sometimes, and that's not all bad. A little bit of stress can give a person energy to do the things they want to do.

But stress is bad when it is more than a little bit—when it starts to make us have an unsettled heart and a troubled spirit.

What can you do when you feel the bad kind of stress? Here are some suggested don'ts and do's:

Don't sit and watch TV or hang out in front of the computer. That can just make things worse.

Don't get angry and kick and break things, or start blaming your brother or sister for the way you feel!

Do ask your mom or dad if you can go outside and breathe some fresh air, and maybe get some exercise! Perhaps you just want to be quiet for a while; maybe even lie in the grass and smell the fragrances of the outdoors.

Do tell someone you are sorry if you have hurt their feelings. It will make you feel a lot better! Or just say some kind words to someone in your family. Making other people happy is a great stress-reliever.

Do listen to some relaxing music and maybe work with your hands on a project or hobby.

Do slow down! Do you have a pet? Just sit with your pet awhile and enjoy how cool animals are. Don't have a pet? Look at a book or a photo album of your family. Breathe deeply and try to let out all that tension!

And most importantly, remember you have a Friend, Jesus, who will always be glad to hear you pray to Him and ask for help when you feel that ready-to-burst feeling coming on!

Conclusion

*One can never consent to creep
when one feels the impulse to soar.*
HELEN KELLER

Oh, oh, oh! Let's go fly a kite, up to the highest height! So began the introduction of this book. Yet, in these pages, you have read some pretty down-to-earth stuff. I hope you are going away with the conviction that it is in mastering the in-the-trenches realities of life that the soaring can really happen.

Special kids, like all kids, have the "impulse to soar," as expressed so well in our Helen Keller quote. But the process of learning to spread those potential wings is often in the context of really difficult realities of life, realities which seem to leave these kids quite heavy and earthbound. Those who care for them can find themselves in the same situation, or at the very least, in a perpetual holding pattern.

Eagles' Wings

I have sought in these chapters to delve into practical ways of dealing with these difficult realities while at the same time turning our attention to the God who promises:

He gives strength to those who are tired; to the ones who lack power, he gives renewed energy. Even youths get tired and weary; even strong young men clumsily stumble.
But those who wait for the Lord's help find renewed strength; they rise up as if they had eagles' wings.
Isaiah 40:29-31, (NET)

Some kids may never walk or run on this present earth, some may never be able to communicate in a typical way, but all are given the invitation to know the God who can make their spirit fly "as if they had eagles' wings."

Mike and I have seen this "flying" in our children. "How can a child be so resilient after suffering so much?" we would wonder. And we have experienced this "soaring" in our own hearts, in dark times, in crushingly hard times. Likely, so have you. And as we grow, we and our children can experience those wings more consistently, more in the day-in-and-day-out circumstances of our lives.

They are wings made up of the knowledge that what is important lies on the inside of each person, that what "the world" values in terms of beauty, talent, success is not what life is made of. Don't these things so quickly pass away? Yet, the qualities of a person's soul can just grow and grow with time. And as character grows, so do abilities in every area of life; so that when we teach our kids to use these wings of faith, we also help them to become all that they were created to be, to bring out the gifts and the unique reflection of God's image that reside in their soul, and to leave a positive mark on the world in which they live.

Our children have an impulse to soar, an un-special need to soar, because deep inside they know that they are important, important to their Creator and important in the grand scheme of things. On the surface, it's often hard for all of us to believe how significant we are; yet way down deep, we know it's true. And God confirms that it is true in His Word through David the psalmist:

> *I look at the heavens you made with your hands.*
> *I see the moon and the stars you created.*
> *And I wonder, "**Why are people so important to you?***
> *Why do you even think about them?*
> *Why do you care so much about humans?*
> *Why do you even notice them?"*
> *But you made them almost like gods*
> *and crowned them with glory and honor.*
>
> Psalm 8:3-5, (ERV)

Notes and Resources

This section is a hybrid of bibliography notes combined with some great resources for you as a parent of a child who has special issues. In many of the notes, we went against conventional formatting for bibliography notes in order to make them more useful for finding what you are looking for. For example, we might give the website address and suggest what to search for when you get to the website home page. In most cases, we have not shared the URL as these seem to change from time to time.

Please note that in sharing these books, websites, and blogs, the author and Special Heart ministry do not necessarily recommend all the content that you may find in any given resource. We endorse the parts of articles, blogs, and book excerpts that are actually quoted in the book.

All website and blog resources were confirmed to still be active in September 2014.

Chapter 1: *I Need a Sense of Purpose*

1. "Interview with Dr. Temple Grandin." *Autism Research Institute*. Interview conducted by Dr. Stephen Edelson. www.autism.com, February 1, 1996.
   (search: interviews. On interview page, search "Temple Grandin")

2. *Biography: Temple Grandin, Ph.D.* (www.grandin.com/temple.html)

3. Susan B. Noyes, "Temple Grandin's 13 Tenets for Raising Successful Children." *Make It Better, North Shore—Family, Community and You,* June 2014. (www.makeitbetter.net (search: "Temple Grandin"))

4. Alan Goldberg and Lauren Putrino, "Teen Locked in Autistic Body Finds Inner Voice." *ABC News*, August 6, 2009. (search: Carly Fleischman abc news)

Chapter 2: *I Need to Be Part of a Healthy Family*

1. Brittany Fichter, "Why Children with Autism Need Holiday Traditions." *Brittany Fichter Blog*: brittanyfichterwrites.com, December 13, 2013. (search: autism holiday traditions)

2. Jay Payleitner, *52 Things Kids Need from a Dad* (Eugene, OR: Harvest House, 2010), 49.

3. *The Family Dinner Project.* thefamilydinnerproject.org/about-us/

4. "How Does a Child with Autism Affect Family Life?" *Care.com*, home page.
   (Scroll down on home page to see quotes from chapter 2.)

5. Gina Demillo Wagner, "Having a Special Needs Brother Does Not Make Me Lucky." *Special Kids.* specialkids.co.za (search: Gina Demillo Wagner)

6. "How Does a Child with Autism Affect Family Life?" *Care.com,* home page.

7. Amy Baskin, "How to Keep Your Relationship Strong While Parenting a Special Needs Child." *Today's Parent,* June 20, 2012.
    (search: Amy Baskin) You will find a ton of her writings here! Once at her page, search the title you are interested in, including the title in this note. Amy's post is derived from an article by Laura Marshak.

8. "Divorce and the Special Needs Parent." *The Thinking Mom's Revolution,* January 21, 2013. (posted by "Professor") http://thinkingmomsrevolution.com/divorce-and-the-special-needs-parent/

9. Daniel, Stetanski, *How to Talk to an Autistic Kid* (Minneapolis, MN: Free Spirit Publishing, 2011)

10. *The Goops* books, originally published beginning in 1900, were created by Gelett Burgess.

Chapter 3: *I Need a Personal Faith in God*

1. Philip Yancey, *Disappointment with God* (Grand Rapids, MI: Zondervan, 1988).

2. Joni Eareckson Tada, *Heaven: Your Real Home* (Grand Rapids, MI: Zondervan, 1995), 53.

3. C.S. Lewis, *The Joyful Christian* (New York, NY: Macmillan, 1977/First Touchstone Edition, 1996), 138.

4.   C.S. Lewis, *The Last Battle* (New York, NY: Harper Collins, 1956), 228.

5.   Anne Graham Lotz, *Heaven: God's Promise for Me* (Grand Rapids, MI: Zondervan, 2011).

Chapter 4: *I Need to Be a Friend*

1.   Temple Grandin and Sean Barron, *The Unwritten Rules of Social Relationships* (Arlington, TX: Future Horizons, 2005).

2.   Ibid., p 74.

3.   Ibid., p 76.

4.   Helen Keller, *The Story of My Life* (Garden City, NY: Doubleday and Page Co., 1914).

5.   William Gibson, *The Miracle Worker* (New York, NY: Simon and Schuster Inc., 1956).

Chapter 5: *I Need to Know That My Parents Delight in Me*

1.   Marcus Buckingham, *Now, Discover Your Strengths* (New York, NY: The Free Press, 2001).

2.   Larry Crabb, *Connecting* (Nashville, TN: Thomas Nelson, 1997).

Chapter 6: *I Need Loving Correction*

1. Michelangelo Buonarroti, "A Poem to Giovanni da Pistoia When the Author Was Painting the Vault of the Sistine Chapel," 1509.
   Note: There are many and various translations of this poem from Italian.

2. Charles Swindoll, *Day by Day with Charles Swindoll* (Nashville, TN: Thomas Nelson, 2000), Week 1, Day 5.

3. Wendy Murray Zoba, "In Memory of Ruth Bell Graham," *Christianity Today,* June 14, 2007.
   www.christianitytoday.com/gifted-for-leadership/2007/june/in-memory-of-ruth-bell-graham.html

4. Anne Graham Lotz, *Heaven: God's Promise for Me* (Grand Rapids, MI: Zondervan, 2011), from the introduction of the book.

5. Henry Cloud and John Townsend, *Boundaries with Kids* (Grand Rapids, MI: Zondervan, 1998), 127.

6. Belinda Letchford's blog: *Live Life with Your Kids!* livelifewithyourkids.wordpress.com

7. Henry Cloud, *Changes That Heal* (Grand Rapids, MI: Zondervan, 2003), 26.

8. Martha C. White, "You Spend Over $1,300 a Year Bribing Your Kids," Time Subscribe, July 16, 2014.

9. Laura Markham, "How to Handle Your Anger at Your Child." *Aha! Parenting,* 2014.
   www.ahaparenting.com / From home page, go to: parenting tips/peaceful parenting.

Chapter 7: *I Need to Learn to Have a Peaceful Heart*

1. *The American Heritage Dictionary.* ahdictionary.com From home page, do a word search: worry.

2. Elisabeth Elliot, *The Journals of Jim Elliot* (Grand Rapids, MI: Revell, 1978)

3. Nicole Watt, "Have We Forgotten the Power of Touch?" Christianity Today, June 5, 2014. From home page go to: Christianity Today tab/her.menuetics/search article

4. Editors of ADDitude Magazine. "An ADHD Cure? Mother Nature Does Her Best to Help Symptoms." ADDitude/ Strategies and Support for ADHD and LD. www.additudemag.com / From home page, go to: mother nature's remedy

5. Helen Keller, *The Story of My Life* (Garden City, NY: Doubleday and Page Co., 1914), Part I, Chapter V.

6. Helen Keller, *The Beauty I Have Seen in Life* (American Foundation for the Blind, Helen Keller Archives, 1938).

Bev's Journey with Jesus

"Do you want to ask Jesus into your life?" Joy asked me this question on a Friday night at a "Christian coffee house" when I was seventeen years old. The music and testimonies being concluded, she spotted me as a visitor and darted over as fast as she could. "Yes, but not tonight," said I. "Oh, but the Bible says, 'Today is the day of salvation,' if you don't do it tonight, you may not do it at all." Amazingly, I had a sense that she was exactly right. So after she briefly explained what it meant to ask Christ into one's life, I bowed my head with her and prayed. She gave me a *Good News for Modern Man* Bible with big print.

What made me so open to this bold invitation from a stranger? A couple things. First, six months earlier on February 9, 1971 at 6:00 a.m., I had been in a pretty major earthquake of 6.6. I was sitting on a bathroom counter putting on some makeup, and although they say that the earthquake only lasted twelve seconds, by the time I frantically reached a doorway to stand in, I was able to surmise that this was the end of the world that I had heard tell of in my Catholic catechism class years ago. I felt what it feels like to not be ready to meet God!

The other thing that made me so open to Joy's invitation to receive Christ was that about a week before I met her, I had walked about four miles round-trip to a Catholic church, thinking that God only heard a person if she prayed in church, and asked God to help me. I was aware of a deep emptiness in my soul, and a wrong direction in my life. I walked back home with no word from Him. But when I got this invitation at the coffee house, I had to wonder, "Is this God's answer?" And indeed it was.

The day after receiving the Bible from Joy, being the seventeen-year-old I was with not much to do on that hot August summer morning, I went down to the pool at the apartments where I lived with my parents in the San Fernando Valley, got in, laid that big Bible on the edge of the pool, and read the entire gospel of John without ever getting out of the water, save for a few food and bathroom breaks. Some neighbors asked me what in the world I was doing. "Nothing. I'm reading a Bible."

But in my own mind and heart, I was astounded because I had tried to read the Bible before, and it seemed to be a bunch of "begets and begats," as my Uncle Buddy used to say. But today.... today, it came alive to me! And I knew that something earth-shattering had happened in my soul. The earthquake months ago was rather symbolic of the shaking up in my being that I was experiencing by having Christ enter my life! Only rather than being destructive, it was a shaking up that I could sense was causing healing and repair.

That night, I went with some friends to a different Christian coffee house. Those were the days in the '70s when the "Jesus people" meant business. Unlike the night before, I felt less like an outsider and more like I was hungry to know more. Someone in front sang a song by Chuck Girard:

Little country church on the edge of town;
People comin' everyday from miles around
for meetin's and for Sunday school;
And it's very plain to see,
It's not the way it used to be...

Long hair, short hair, some coats and ties;
People finally comin' around;
Lookin' past the hair and straight into the eyes;
People finally comin' around!

These people were excited about their faith, and much to my amazement, I was excited about my new faith too!

Later someone read me *The Four Spiritual Laws*, which told me more clearly what I had done the night before: I had repented of my sin and accepted Christ's death on the cross, making Him my Savior.

There was a movement going on, and I was caught right in the middle of it. Thank God that I was!

I didn't have any plans for college, even though I had just finished high school. There wasn't any encouragement from my home to pursue any such endeavors. So from about seventh grade until the time I graduated high school, I drifted. I took the easiest classes available just to get through, and I got into the Southern California teen lifestyle, which was not healthy, to say the least.

After my encounter with Christ and His people, my parents were amazed at the change in me, and at first, they actually feared that I was in a cult. I guess it was that kind of spacey, "I can't believe how happy I am" look that I had. But over time, especially when I started telling them that the Bible said I was supposed to honor my parents, they relaxed. My dad remained an atheist at that time, but my mom, who was raised Catholic, and my older brother both got into the whole thing, and what a change came about in our previously very dysfunctional family!

My dad was working as a gardener at a community college during this time, and since registration was near, and I suppose since he saw this change in me, he took it upon himself to talk to the dean of the college, who got me into fall registration on the very first day, giving me first priority choice of classes.

So there I was in college. And oh, how I felt the pain now of taking all those "bonehead" classes in high school. In biology, I couldn't even focus my microscope, while the others students seemed to know exactly what to do. And I'd never seen algebra before, so it took hours each night to study and pass with a B! But I was in college, and doing pretty well, under the circumstances.

The most surprising thing was when I got to my English classes. I'd never had any college prep classes, not even close. Yet, when I was assigned college-level work to write long papers, I got As without much effort, or even knowing exactly what I was doing.

Are you starting to see God's providence in my life? He had a plan for me all along...a plan to share His truth and His love within a certain context, and writing was part of that plan, so He gave me the abilities I needed in a beyond-natural way!

Not too long into my college experience, I came in contact with a Christian group who discipled me and taught me more how to live the Christian life and how to share it with others.

I remember my health class. One of the young men in there used to call me "Sunshine" because I was very verbal about my joy in my newfound faith. In that class was a student named Karen Leonard. One day after class, I passed by the pinball machines; there was Karen playing a game, and I asked her if I could share with her how to become a Christian. She said, yes, after her game was over. She prayed with me to receive Christ. Karen contributed to this book that you have in your hands in chapter 5, which tells you that this pinball encounter was the beginning of a very significant relationship! More about Karen, in a moment...

So when I wasn't studying, I was learning to help other young women grow in their faith. Let me tell you about some of these college women:

There was Candy, whom I met in my tennis class. Candy had protracted spinal meningitis when she was young, and as a result, her left side from her face down to her toes was weak and malformed. Our tennis teacher pulled me aside one day and told me that I had to rotate partners because I was never going to learn tennis if I only played with Candy. In spite of the reality that I chased the tennis ball most of the class hour, I said, "I'll learn; I'll learn." And learn I did, against the backboards after my classes many days! Candy prayed to receive Christ with me and attended church with me for quite a while. And we both got As in our tennis class!

There was also Valerie. Valerie was completely blind. I met her when I was attending California State University at Northridge. We would meet weekly to go over a Bible study and other material to help her grow in her faith. Once when I was walking from the college campus to her dorm which was down a major street, someone threw a McDonald's glass of Coke at me from a car window. I was drenched with sticky Coke from head to toe. I called Val and told her we had to cancel. She would not hear of it, and begged me to come for Bible study time. It meant a lot to her. So after I showered, I met with her after all. I eventually got to meet Val's family, a Jewish family, and get acquainted with some of Val's hidden talents. For example, she was an accomplished pianist!

Then there were Betty, who had a form of dwarfism; Carol, who was deaf; and Marsha, who had learning disabilities.

Again, I see God's providence, because I did not seek out these women who had special needs; they were just in my path at the right time in the right place. I don't know of any other individuals who had special needs who were involved with the Christian group I was with. God sent them all my way...because He had something in mind for me to do in my future.

This was part of my journey with Jesus. He knew that later I would have children of my own with special needs. And He knew that Karen Leonard also would have a son who had special issues. He also knew that He would put in both of our hearts a burning desire to make God's love known to special-needs families.

And far away, in Illinois, was a young man whom I was yet to meet, and whom God was also preparing for our life together in His own special way.

That is the beginning of my journey with Jesus, a journey that had an intentional plan, a work of sovereign providence from the very beginning. Because with God, nothing is random; nothing is a mistake.

> *You will make known to me the path of life;*
> *In Your presence is fullness of joy.*
> Psalm 16:11

Follow Bev on Twitter @BevLinder

Reach Higher!

Un-Special Needs was written as an encouragement to parents of kids who have special issues to look up, to further realize the God-given potential of their kids and of themselves as parents, and to embrace what *is*, rather than "what could have been." Now there is a tool especially crafted to help parents go deeper and to reach higher.

Leader's Guide Included

Jim and Karen Leonard wrote the workbook that accompanies *Un-Special Needs* with a goal of reaching further into the concepts of the book with additional scripture as well as plenty of enjoyable, thought-provoking activities and group discussion opportunities. This tool is perfect for both individual study and group interaction.

For information on ordering the book/workbook combination or the workbook alone, go to:

www.special-heart.com

Also available separately on Amazon.com

18539285R00100

Made in the USA
San Bernardino, CA
18 January 2015